rock'n'roll jews

Judaic Traditions in Literature, Music, and Art
Ken Frieden *and* Harold Bloom, *eds.*

michael billig

rock 'n' roll

jews

SYRACUSE UNIVERSITY PRESS

First Syracuse University Press Edition 2001

06   6 5 4 3 2

Originally published by Five Leaves Publications in 2000.

The paper used in this publication meets the minimum requirements
of American National Standard for Information Sciences—Permanence
of Paper for Printed Library Materials, NSI Z39.48-1984.∞™

Library of Congress Cataloging-in-Publication Data

Billig, Michael.
Rock 'n' roll Jews / Michael Billig.
p. cm.—(Judaic traditions in literature, music, and art)
ISBN 0-8156-0705-9 (pbk.)
1. Jewish musicians. 2. Blacks—Relations with Jews. 3. Rock
music—History and criticism. I. Title: Rock and roll Jews. II. Title.
III. Series.
ML3776 .B53 2001
781.66'089'924—dc21
2001018360

Manufactured in the United States of America

Contents

Preface to the American Edition

It gives me great pleasure as an author to see that *Rock-'n'Roll Jews* now has an American edition. The book may have been written and first published in England, but essentially it is a book about American music and about the hidden Jewish contribution to that music. It is becoming increasingly common this side of the Atlantic to sneer at American popular culture. 'Hollywood', 'Disney', and 'Coca-Cola' are all used as adjectives of criticism. When Europeans call a film 'pure Hollywood', you can hear the tone of disdain. In this mood of superiority, it is easy to overlook the wondrous nature of American popular music in the past hundred years. From no other nation has come such a variety and vibrancy of music for ordinary people. This music—jazz, blues, boogie, country, rock— has spoken directly to many millions around the world. If this is cultural colonialism, so be it: this is a colonialism of enjoyment.

Rock'n'roll in its early days was, above all, American. Anyone in Britain, growing up in the years before the Beatles and the Stones, would know how thinly feeble the British copies sounded, as did the continental clones of Elvis in France and Italy. The American records were the real thing. It was as if the dangerous rural south of the States was spreading across the Atlantic, sweeping away old world stuffiness. What now appears surprising is that urban Jews, who seemed to represent the very antithesis of rock, contributed so much to this magic music.

The Jewish contribution was massive, but *Rock'n'Roll Jews,* which charts that contribution, is short. Inevitably, there has had to be selection. Because people care about popular music—it is *their* music after all—some readers have been upset that their particular favourites have been given all too little space, or have even been omitted altogether. The book does not aim to be an encyclopaedia of Jews in modern popular music. Perhaps someone will write a wider history which will continue the history of Jews in rock through the 70s and into the twenty-first century. Unlike *Rock'n'Roll Jews,* which concentrates on rock's early history, such a book will make space for Marc Bolan's tragic story, for Steely Dan's Donald Fagen and Walter Becker, for Kiss and Gene Simmons (born Chaim Witz), for the Beastie Boys, for . . . the list continues. And readers of the American edition will have their own suggestions.

Even in the period covered by the book, however, there had to be omissions and simplifications. There was a story to tell, rather than a list to complete. Some omissions I now regret. I should have found space to mention Art Rupe (né Arthur Goldberg) who produced Little Richard's great hits and many of Sam Cooke's early gospel songs on Speciality Records. And the story behind Elvis's coming to record his version of Leiber and Stoller's 'Hound Dog' was more complicated than is presented here. Because many of the readers care about the music, they have collected and treasured factual details over the years. Yes, Paul Simon's 'Me And Julio Down By The Schoolyard' was on the 1972 album, contrary to what is written in chapter six. I only hope is that such oversights do not upset the general tale.

So, as author, I plead for tolerance from fellow lovers of this music. *Rock'n'Roll Jews* might aim to analyse the Jewish contribution—to say why it occurred and why it has been overlooked—but it also seeks to be a work of celebration. It celebrates some special people, like Doc Pomus and Jerry Ragovoy, who created some special music that I for one have never wished to outgrow.

February 2001   Michael Billig

rock'n'roll jews

Acknowledgements

Writing this book has been a pleasure, quite unlike some of the more narrowly academic books that I have written in the past. I have been able to write as an *amateur*, in the original sense of the word. Literally, an *amateur* does something out of love rather than for professional reasons. In my case, I have been writing principally as a lover of early rock music, not as an academic social scientist. In fact, much social scientific writing about rock is rather cumbersome, burying the sounds under a heap of difficult words. I have avoided the heavy jargon. Nevertheless, in tracing the Jewish origins of much rock music, I have inevitably drawn upon my training in the social sciences. For this is a story about culture, prejudice and identity — all things I have written about in the past, sometimes using the heavy words of social science to do so.

A number of thanks are due. First I would like to thank Ross Bradshaw of Five Leaves. He originally suggested that I write a short pamphlet on the Jewish contribution to rock. As the manuscript grew to book size, Ross, far from complaining, continued to offer suggestions about singers and episodes that I'd neglected. Ross got to know of my interest in the topic following a talk which I gave to the Nottingham Council of Christians and Jews. I would like to thank Danny Donen for the invitation and for suggesting, along with other members of the audience, that I work up the talk for publication.

A number of academic friends and colleagues read early drafts and made helpful suggestions. In particular, I am grateful to Charles Antaki, Graham Murdock, and Mike

1

Pickering — all colleagues of mine in the Department of Social Sciences at Loughborough University. I would also like to thank Susan Condor, grand-daughter of Harry 'There's An Organ Playing In My Dreams' Cohen.

Finally, there's my family. My children have been pleased that, finally, after all these years, I was writing about something vaguely interesting. Daniel, Rebecca, Rachel and Ben have read parts of the manuscript, made suggestions and offered their own comments. I am grateful to them, and also to Sheila with whom, at home and on long car journeys, I have been able to share, amongst many other things, a love of Jewish rock music.

Jews in Rock: a Hidden Story

'The Jewish contribution to rock'n'roll' does not appear to be a serious topic. It sounds more like the opening line of an old Jewish joke. There is a scene in the spoof movie *Airplane*, when a passenger asks for some light reading and is given 'The Complete Guide to Jewish Sporting Stars'. It turns out to be a blank sheet of paper. One can imagine the joke being applied to rock'n'roll stars. Jewish crooners? Whole books could be, and have been, written. Jewish psychologists? There could be whole sections in libraries. Jewish rock'n'roll stars? Just turn the empty pages.

The most famous and the wildest of the early rock'n'roll stars had strong roots in the deep Christian south of the States. Elvis Presley was brought up to attend church regularly. Little Richard learnt to sing in gospel choirs and later, when his career had faltered, he became a preacher. As for Jerry Lee Lewis, he seems to have spent his whole life wrestling with the devil.

Chuck Berry, in his classic rock song 'Johnny B. Goode', describes the poor boy, who dreams of being a rock star and seeing his name in lights. The song, which has become a virtual anthem for every would-be rock star, depicts the boy living in a country shack in some remote, rural area of the States. The dreaming wannabe is not a city boy, studying for his Bar Mitzvah under the watch of ambitious parents. That would not fit the image. 'Johnny B. Goode' is the fictional cultural hero of rock, not 'Jonathan B. Goldstein'.

Then, if one turns to the other side of the Atlantic, the situation appears similar. The most obvious British stars

3

from rock's premier division are certainly not Jewish. Neither the Beatles nor the Rolling Stones would provide Jewish names to add to the blank sheet. At first sight, therefore, rock would seem to be the music of poor Southerners from the United States—whether black or white—perhaps distilled through working-class Liverpudlians or rude, street-wise Londoners.

However, appearances can be deceptive. There is a hidden story about the central Jewish contribution waiting to be told. This is not a story of uncovering forgotten Jewish ancestors. There will be no revelations that Elvis or Little Richard had Jewish great-great-grandmothers. Even if such ancestry could be found, it would hardly be significant. After all, rock'n'roll was not created by forgotten, long dead, great-great-grandmothers.

Nor will the story of the overlooked Jewish contribution depend upon a trawl through rock's minor celebrities. In fact, the blank sheet could be partially filled with a respectable collection of reasonably well-known names. There could be Marc Bolan, Manfred Mann and Peter Green, who was Fleetwood Mac's original, and arguably most talented, guitarist. We could then move forward to take in the Beastie Boys and Ian Broudie of the Lightning Seeds. And so on. But the resulting compilation would not be a premier division list. It would lack the founding performers — the Elvises, the Jerry Lees, the Chucks, not to mention the John, Paul, George and Ringos.

However, searching for Jewish band-members from the early days to the present would not be the way to document the immense Jewish contribution to rock. In fact, if one concentrated upon the public performers, one would almost entirely miss the core of the Jewish contribution. At least in rock's early days, that contribution lay behind the scenes, largely hidden from the public gaze.

Of course, managers and impresarios operate behind the scenes. In the world of show business, there have been Jewish managers aplenty. In fact, the very word 'rock-'n'roll' itself was the creation of rock's earliest and most

4

famous promoter, Alan Freed. It is said that he even tried to copyright the term. However, a history of rock's Jewish contribution which concentrated on management would tend to confirm the blank sheet of paper. The contribution would not be a creative one, but one which facilitates the creativity of others, who would be the real heroes of rock's story. Indeed, even Freed's claim to have linguistically invented 'rock'n'roll' has been disputed.

There is, however, a contribution which is both behind-the-scenes and also highly creative. When thinking of classic rock'n'roll, it is easy just to think of the performers—to imagine Elvis in his gold suit, or Jerry Lee, pounding the piano with his hair flopping forward. What can be forgotten is that these performers often did not write their own songs.

Moreover, the young rock fans were principally linked to the stars, not by public performances, but by records. Millions, who had never seen Elvis perform, could buy his records. For the average teenager, this was the way to be a fan. Elvis's records, and those of the other rock stars, sounded different from anything that the previous generation had ever listened to. The whine of the electric guitar, the crisp drumming, the echo effects, and, later, more complex mixtures of electric and acoustic instruments all made rock'n'roll a new sound. This was modern music, made in a modern way.

Someone had to write the songs. Someone had to create the sounds. If Elvis didn't compose his own words and music, then he certainly didn't produce his own records. Who were these hidden composers? Who were the behind-the-scenes producers who crafted the new ways of creating music?

Once these questions are asked, then the Jewish names come tumbling out. Names such as Jerry Leiber, Mike Stoller, Doc Pomus, Jerry Wexler, Jerry Ragovoy and Phil Spector — these are the real heroes of this book. Rock fans will know songs like 'Hound Dog', 'Jailhouse Rock', 'Save The Last Dance For Me', 'You've Lost That Lovin'

Feelin'", 'Sweets For My Sweet' and many, many more.

For a whole generation, such songs marked the times in which they grew up. The music was part of life and the sounds continue to haunt the memory. Years later the songs are instantly recognizable, often from the first bar, even the first note, of the classic recording. You only have to hear Elvis start to sing unaccompanied 'You ain't' to know that 'nothing but a hound dog' is to follow.

Yet how many people, who grew up in the fifties or sixties, would be able to name the composers? More to the point, how many young Jewish boys or girls who listened to such music, often with severe parental disapproval, would know that, in a literal sense, they were hearing 'Jewish music'?

The Jewish contribution does not end there. The early history of rock can be divided into two periods of roughly ten years each. It would be easiest to label these periods the music of the fifties and that of the sixties. But, strictly speaking, that would be inaccurate. During the first part of the fifties, the music of the forties was still going strong. Rock'n'roll did not make its rude entrance until the mid-fifties. The first period lasted from about 1955 to 1965. This was the period when the Jewish songwriters and producers made their greatest and most innovative contributions. At first, this contribution was to be found with the sounds of classic rock and rhythm and blues. Then it softened into lighter, poppier songs, as strings were used to complement the electric guitars.

The second period starts with the rise of the Beatles and the Stones. This is the music of the sixties, although, musically speaking, 'sixties music' did not really get going until about 1964. This was a time of change and protest, which made the fifties, by contrast, seem nostalgically quiet. Fashions altered dramatically: boys' hair grew longer in the sixties while girls' skirts shortened. Freedom and rebellion were in the air. Illegal substances were smoked. Taboos were publicly broken. There were large-scale demonstrations against authority, including, of course, mass political demonstrations against the Vietnam war, against the running of universities and against racist segregation in the south of the United States.

Not surprisingly in a time of political and cultural change, the sounds of pop music developed. In this new era, the back-room composers lost their supreme niche as so many of the new singers were writing their own material. Indeed they were expected to do so. Pop was changing. A more educated, middle-class type of person was beginning to use rock as a means of expression. More complex, even poetic, lyrics were being written. Here again, there was a solid Jewish contribution. Foremost among the singer-songwriters of this era we find Bob Dylan, Paul Simon, Lou Reed and Leonard Cohen — all raised as Jews and all, indelibly, leaving a mark on their times.

What counts in all this are numbers. One notable figure proves little. The fact that Bob Dylan was Jewish does not in itself suggest anything about the relations between Jews and popular music. But the fact that Paul Simon, Lou Reed and Leonard Cohen's names can also be added indicates that here might be something of more historical and cultural significance. It is the same with the names of composers and producers of rock's first decade.

One Jew writing hit songs might be of interest to family and the local Jewish press. Two Jews — and the professional anti-semites start to get interested, suspecting a conspiracy. Three Jews — this might just be a sign of a wider cultural trend. In the case of rock's early history, the numbers involved are well beyond the level of chance.

The point can be illustrated in relation to country and western music. It would be possible to find a few individual Jews who have made contributions. Most notably, the late Shel Silverstein, former New York cartoonist, playwright and author of children's books, also wrote some spoof country songs. In fact, the spoofs became popular with genuine country music performers, who have always understood the power of irony and self-parody. Silverstein provided Johnny Cash with his biggest UK single hit, 'A

Boy Named Sue'. He also wrote hits for other country singers such as Loretta Lynn and Bobby Bare, not to mention providing a stream of hits for Dr Hook, including the wonderfully witty 'Sylvia's Mother'. But one Jew amongst the sons and daughters of southern Baptists is not enough to say that country music has significant New York Jewish roots. Similarly, the fact that the country singer Charley Pride is black does not establish country music as black music. Nor does it wipe away the racist past of much country music. To make such cases, much more is required than the occasional maverick, however talented he or she might be.

For this reason, the present strategy is not to take the long trawl to compile an extensive 'Encyclopaedia Judaica of Rock'. Some figures will be omitted. There will be no discussion of Marc Bolan or the Beastie Boys. Nor will there be agonizing discussion about whether someone like Mark Knopfler qualifies for inclusion on the basis of a Jewish father. Technical discussions about the definition of Jewishness can be left to rabbinic authorities. For present purposes, it is not completeness that matters, but identifying the points at which significant numbers of Jewish contributions were made.

Identifying the contribution is one thing. But further questions arise. Why did Jews play such a role? And, most interestingly, why has this role remained hidden? The histories of rock, whether academic or glossily popular, certainly don't draw attention to the Jewish aspect. In order to answer such questions — or, to be more precise, to begin to offer answers — one must do more than name names and compile lists. One must set rock in a wider cultural context.

Above all, one must set the history of rock in the context of race relations, especially in the United States. Most obviously, this means examining the relations between blacks and whites, and asking whether white performers such as Elvis were merely ripping off black musicians. This question is a familiar one. Certainly the academic histories of rock do not avoid it. In fact, they are obsessed by it.

However, ethnic relations are not merely a matter of black and white. There are shades of sallow too. In order to understand the Jewish contribution, one must go back to a time in recent American history before ethnicity was something to be publicly displayed, especially by performing artistes. In the 1950s, but also well into the 1960s, America, in its public display, seemed to be a White Anglo-Saxon Protestant culture. Heroes and heroines had suitably blond hair and creamy skin. This was a time singers could have hits with titles such as 'Pretty Blue Eyes'. Tommy Roe, with his massive hit in 1962, could rhapsodise about his 'Sheila' with her "blues eyes and pony-tail".

White suburban teenagers might have innocently hummed along to such catchy tunes. Even today, the words and melodies express an era of uncomplicated naivety. 'Pretty Blue Eyes' and 'Sheila' will find their way onto the sound tracks of retro, nostalgic movies which aim to re-capture those times, with images of boys with quiffs, girls with back-combed hair and cars with wide tail-fins. But beware the innocence: race is never far from the surface of American cultural history. All these references to the desirable beauty of blue eyes, blonde hair and pony-tails exclude African Americans. Chuck Berry, for one, was well aware of this. His 'Brown-Eyed Handsome Man' was an explicit riposte to all the blue-eyed sentimentality.

It was not just African Americans who were excluded by the WASPish ideal. Statistically many Jews and Italians have failed to fit the Aryan, blond, blue-eyed model — although pony-tails are less of a problem. In those distant times, it didn't pay to be too swarthy, if one wished to be a performing star. Or more particularly, it did not pay to be outwardly Jewish in appearance. After all, Elvis had a hint of swarthiness and he dyed his hair jet black: that darkness was vital for his early bad-boy image. But Elvis could never be mistaken for a Jew. In the fifties, 'too Jewish' was a term of criticism, used significantly both by Jews and non-Jews.

At first glance, this might sound over-stretched, even paranoid. However, rock music is only one part of a wider entertainment industry. The simultaneous contribution and public exclusion of Jews has been well documented in the film industry. Neal Gabler, in his book *An Empire Of Their Own*, has shown how Hollywood was virtually created by Jews. First generation immigrants, such as Louis B. Mayer, Adolph Zukor and Jack Warner, re-invented themselves as Americans and, in so doing, they created their own image of the American dream[1]. They used suitably WASPish actors and their films did not present Jewish themes. During the 1930s there were few Jewish film actors, although the ownership and senior management of the studies were dominated by Jews. There were Jewish scriptwriters and directors by the hundreds. Gabler quotes one Jewish screenwriter, Maurice Rapf, mentioning how Jewish film-actors, if they made it to Hollywood, did not publicly advertise their Jewishness:

> *"There were some hidden Jews. Not that in their private life they made any secret of it. But they were not known to the general public, and the studios didn't want it known, either."*[2]

By the time rock emerged, the situation in the film industry had not changed dramatically. By now there were some Jewish stars. But in the main they had changed their names, accents and gestures. Certainly, the bulk of the Jewish talent was kept behind scenes, away from the public gaze. The same pattern, it will be suggested, can be found in the early history of rock'n'roll.

---

1. Gabler, N. (1989) *An Empire Of Their Own: how the Jews invented Hollywood*. New York: Anchor Books.
2. Gabler, p301.

The sixties, which supposedly was a time when old taboos were discarded, and new freedoms championed, did not change everything. Even then, one can find Jewish singer-songwriters reinventing themselves as all-Americans and in the process reconstructing an American folk history, just as the old movie moguls had done. The inhibitions against appearing 'too Jewish' were not fully extinguished. The culture of prejudice did not suddenly sink without trace.

But why should Jews have been attracted to the job of writing rock songs in the first place? It will be suggested that, in part, this reflects a continuation of the Jewish tradition of popular songwriting. Hollywood was not all that those early immigrants to the United States created. Tin Pan Alley, too, was principally a Jewish creation. The networks and cultural traditions of Tin Pan Alley were to continue to be important, at least in the early days of rock'n'roll.

The history of anti-semitism also cannot be ignored. The twentieth century simultaneously witnessed the worst persecution of Jews in a long history of persecution, and an amazing flowering of creativity. In the arts, sciences and popular culture (excluding, as *Airplane's* joke suggested, athletic sports), the contribution of twentieth century Jews has been incalculable, and certainly out of all proportion to the total numbers of Jews.

The sociologist, Zygmunt Bauman, has offered an explanation for this record of creative achievement. He has used a metaphor, taken from Kafka, to explain this Jewish cultural and scientific renaissance.[3] The Jews in the early part of the twentieth century were, Bauman suggests, like a four-legged animal, caught in the act of leaping. The front legs had already left the ground, but they had not yet found a secure resting place. Jews were leav-

---

3. Bauman, Z. (1992) *Intimations of Postmodernity*. London: Routledge, p227.

ing the enclosed world of the ghetto. They were leaping into the modern world of European cultural life. Yet, that modern world was a dangerous, unwelcoming place for Jews. There was little safe ground on which the leaping animal could land. Caught in this unique situation, Jews responded with a burst of creativity.

The Jews, however, who helped create the songs and sounds of early rock, were growing up in the comparative security of the United States, far from the scene of European persecutions. Some grew up in the poorer parts of New York; some, during their childhood, made the historic journey from city to suburb, and, thereby, from poverty or near poverty to economic security. Others were born in the suburbs, enjoying conditions which their grandparents had aspired to but not achieved.

By and large, the Jews who contributed to rock's history, belonged to a generation that grew up amongst other Jews. As will be seen, Jewish networks are crucial to this story. In their first marriages, members of this generation would have been likely to marry a fellow Jew. But in their second or third marriages they would have been less likely. This generation was keen to embrace the American culture. For this generation, there could be no going back to the ever-weakening traditions of earlier generations. Most of the boys in this generation would have had Bar Mitzvahs. But, when writing songs of childhood and adolescence, this was not something to be mentioned musically. For the Jew in a gentile world, some taboos still remained.

This generation was not living in trouble-free times. Even by the 1950s, anti-semitism was still part of everyday life in the States. The cultural critic, Theodor Adorno, remarked that he encountered more anti-semitism in the United States than he had in pre-war Nazi Germany.[4] Adorno was one of the co-writers of the classic book that

4. Adorno, T.W. (1968) 'Scientific experiences of a European scholar in America', in D. Fleming and B. Bailyn (eds), *The Intellectual Migration*. Cambridge, Mass.: Harvard University Press.

investigated the psychology of post-war American anti-semitism: the study showed that even so-called unprejudiced persons tended to accept the prevalent unflattering stereotypes of Jews.[5] Of course, such prejudices and the routine exclusion from suburban golf clubs, cannot be compared with the violent ferocity which, years earlier, had driven that generation's parents and grandparents from Eastern European ghettos.

The Jews, who helped to create rock, were growing up as Americans but still were catching the tail-ends of a long history of anti-semitism. Their formative years occurred before ethnic identity had become fashionable. Jewishness was not something to be waved around too publicly in a gentile world. This was particularly true in the early fifties, when the rabid anti-communism of the McCarthyite era was still casting its shadow. There was more than an undertow of anti-semitism in McCarthyism, linking Jews with un-American activities, especially in the entertainment industries. As Philip Roth, in his recent novel *I Married a Communist* comments, "the Cold War paranoia had latent anti-semitism as one of its sources".[6] In this climate, as will be seen, being 'too Jewish' was not 'cool', while rock, of course, was very cool.

There is another factor which may help to explain why Jews played a significant part in rock's early days. As has often been said, rock'n'roll was created out of a fusion of musical styles. In particular, it combined the hillbilly country music of poor Southern whites with the blues of

---

5. Adorno, T.W, Frenkel-Brunswik, E., Levinson, D.J. and Sanford, R.N. (1950) *The Authoritarian Personality*. New York: Harper and Row. Adorno also wrote criticisms of popular music, which have become classic analyses for cultural theorists. See, for instance, Adorno, T.W. (1976) *Introduction to the Sociology of Popular Music*. New York: Seabury Press. The problem for cultural theorists is that Adorno clearly despised popular music, while, at the same time, providing powerful theories for analysing mass culture: see, for instance, Middleton, R. (1990) *Studying Popular Music*. Buckingham: Open University Press.
6. Roth, P. (1999) *I Married a Communist*. London: Vintage, p274.

even poorer blacks. The collaboration necessary for this musical fusion was never going to be easy. At the time of rock's emergence, there was still massive segregation in the deep South. There, both blacks and whites were mutually suspicious of each other and of each other's cultural heritages.

Who better, then, to make the fusion than Jews, who were distancing themselves from their own cultural heritages? The music of the synagogue was to play little part in rock's history. By contrast, the Jewish musical innovators could play with the musical heritages of gospel, blues and country music, moving easily from one to another. More than this, such rock composers were continuing the earlier traditions of Jewish Tin Pan Alley songwriters. George Gershwin had the genius to combine the syncopated rhythms of black jazz with European classical traditions, constructing catchy tunes for a mass audience. Similar fusions, it will be suggested, can be found in the works of the great rock composers, such as Leiber and Stoller.

Again, in the second era of rock, Jews were ideally placed to give the old white American folk traditions a rocking boost. They themselves were not really a product of such traditions. So in claiming folk music as their own, they altered it. And in moving easily between different traditions, they were following models set by the great popular Jewish writers of Tin Pan Alley, against whom, ironically, figures such as Dylan saw themselves as rebelling.

All this suggests that there is a hidden story to be told. But a word of caution should be emphasised. This is not a story which has been deliberately hidden and which only now, to quote the phrase much used by popular journalists, can be told to the public. It is a story of not noticing and not wanting to be noticed. But now, as the old prejudices recede and ethnicity becomes something that can be more easily displayed in public, it is possible to draw attention to things that previously were only half-recognized and about which it would have been better not to comment too loudly.

At this stage a personal word is in order. I, too, must confess that until comparatively recently I shared the general ignorance about rock's Jewish contribution. A few years ago, my wife and I were planning the celebration of our younger daughter's Bat Mitzvah. We certainly did not want to hire, at massive expense, the sort of band which specialises in Bar Mitzvah music. Nor did I want to make a tape of Klezmer music, which has experienced a pronounced revival in the 1980s and 1990s. Today there are a number of excellent young Jewish musicians playing this music of Eastern European ghetto life. I have tried to like Klezmer. An ancestral heritage it might be, but it feels alien. 'My' music stubbornly remains the rock and soul of the late fifties and early sixties. The spirit of conscious ethnic revival seems artificial when put against sounds that were the backdrop of so much lived experience.

My wife and I therefore decided that for the Bat Mitzvah celebration I would make a tape of rock music. However, in keeping with the spirit of the occasion, I would limit the tape to songs which had Jewish composers or co-composers. I was expecting to find a few familiar songs here and there. I anticipated that I would have to pad out the tape with quite a bit of Bob Dylan and Paul Simon, hoping to find enough jaunty numbers amongst their works. To my surprise, song after well-known pop song revealed itself to be 'Jewish music', from the music of Presley to the softer sounds of the Drifters and Phil Spector. So much of the rebellious music which I had loved in my youth and which seemed to be a window into a foreign, dangerous world, turned out to be a product of familiar surroundings. Surprise was mingled with pleasure.

From Tin Pan Alley To Rock

2

Soon after I had begun looking at the Jewish contribution to rock-'n'roll, I told an eminent sociologist what I was doing. She was an expert in the sociology of popular culture and had written about rock music herself. Her reaction was revealing. After an initial smile, she exclaimed 'Oh, you mean the background business side'. No, I said. I meant the creative side.

The reaction of my friend shows the extent to which images can become fixed in the mind — even in the minds of experts. In this case, there is the established stereotype of Jewish males as businessmen. There is also the image of the rock star as the very antithesis of the businessman — and certainly not the bookish, bespectacled Jewish 'type'. Put the two stereotypes together, and you have the assumption that Jews might be the managers of rock stars, but they are hardly likely to be rock'n'rollers themselves.

An additional theme seems to confirm the impression. Weren't the great rock'n'rollers men from poor, Southern backgrounds? You can't expect to find many Jews amongst the hillbilly sharecroppers of the Deep South or hanging round the black juke joints of the Mississippi Delta.

The histories of rock'n'roll do little to upset such assumptions. They might discuss at length the relative contributions of African American blues and boogie-woogie music, comparing the influence of black music with white country and western. The popular illustrated histories will typically include grainy black and white photos of the forerunners of rock. There might be pictures of baggy-suited boogie singers such as Big Joe Turner or the

17

pinched features of white country singers like Hank Williams.[1] There won't be a Jewish face in sight.

So it would continue into rock's second era. No illustrated rock history would be complete without a picture of the 'Fab Four', the Beatles, in their heyday. The photos are familiar: four working-class, knowing young men, confident in their collarless suits. Some photos might show a fifth figure — a slightly older, pudgy-faced man in a conventional suit, standing awkwardly to one side and looking recognizably Jewish. Brian Epstein, the Beatles' manager, was the son of a wealthy businessman and highly protective mother. He could never be one of the band. He might envy the Beatles' energy, freedom and mischief-making but he had to remain apart. The nearest he could get was to manage their financial affairs and to advise them on matters of dress. At first sight, that would appear to sum up the Jewish contribution to rock.

Before the rock era it was all very different. If one turns to the early histories of American popular music, one would find books filled with Jewish names and photographs of obviously Jewish faces. The same generation of Jews, who created the Hollywood film industry, also produced what has become known as 'Tin Pan Alley' — the centre of the popular music industry based on Broadway in New York. As one historian of American popular songs has written: Tin Pan Alley was "dominated by Jewish Americans" and it represents "one of the first great contributions to American culture by the New York Jewish community".[2]

The pre-eminence of Tin Pan Alley seemed to be threatened when rock burst onto the scene in the mid-1950s. In the words of the *Rolling Stone* journalist, Mikal

---

1. See, for instance, Tosches, D. (1991) *The Unsung Heroes Of Rock'n'Roll*. London: Secker and Warburg.
2. Hamm, C. (1979) *Yesterdays: popular song in America*. New York: W.W. Norton and Co, p 27.

18

Gilmore, rock'n'roll in the 1950s meant disruption: it was "the clamour of young people, kicking hard".[3] Rock appeared as an aggressive rejection of the style of Tin Pan Alley's music. The sentimentality of crooners, the jolliness of women singing novelty numbers about railways 'running through the middle of the house' and the respectability of tuxedoed band-leaders: all that seemed to be being thrust aside. As Carl Belz wrote in his influential history of rock, early rock was "a protest against the music of the past and of an older generation, and against the values of that generation".[4]

The young were reacting against the complacency of their parents' generation. The parents might like gentle crooners, singing sentimentally about innocent love. These crooners would be accompanied by traditional, non-amplified musical instruments, making harmonious sounds. The generation that had lived through the hard times of depression and the Second World War, preferred its music soft and romantic. Their children, growing up in safer, more affluent times, wanted to hear dangerous music. They responded to simple chords, a jumping beat and loud electric guitars. The music conveyed sex, rather than romance. Thus, rock was never wholly innocent. It was always a rude rebellion. So many parents in the fifties were perplexed. Was it for this that they had fought the war?

The old was being pushed aside. To quote Carl Belz once again, the new rock music "provided an alternative to *kitsch*".[5] Chuck Berry, in the title of one of his most famous songs, celebrated the arrival of rock: 'Roll Over

---

3. Gilmore, M. (1999) *Night Beat: a shadow history of rock & roll*. London: Picador, p23.
4. Belz, C. (1972) *The Story of Rock*. New York: Oxford University Press, p31.
5. Belz, *The Story of Rock*, p. 19. Similarly, Middleton, in *Studying Popular Music*, describes rock'n'roll as a "refusal of sentimentality" and "a radical subversion of the culture represented by Tin Pan Alley" (p43).

19

Beethoven', he sang. In truth it was not really Beethoven or Tchaikovsky who rolled over. Classical music would continue to attract its same, comparatively small, elite audiences.[6] What rolled over was the music that Belz dismissed as *kitsch*. Much of the music that was being pushed aside had a direct, or indirect, Jewish heritage. It was not so much a case of rock ordering Beethoven out of the way, as 'Roll over Show-bizz *Schmaltz*'.

In some respects, as will be seen, the stereotypes are true. The old Tin Pan Alley music had a strong Jewish dimension. The performers of rock were, in the main, men from the margins of society. There were Jewish managers in the rock age, but few Jewish performers. All this is correct. But it is not the full story. The Jewish tradition of popular song-writing did not stop overnight once Elvis burst into song. In fact, many of the key features of Tin Pan Alley's music were to be reproduced in the era of rock.

Jews And Tin Pan Alley

From the early 1880s there was a mass exodus of Jews from eastern Europe, particularly from Tsarist Russia. Between two and three million Jews, over a period of several decades, made their way to the United States. There, they were faced with a mixture of good and bad luck. Their bad luck was that they frequently encountered conditions of extreme poverty. Men and women from small Eastern European towns were crowded into city tenements. The newcomers were hardly welcomed by a Protestant establishment that often shared the European anti-semitic assumptions. Even so, this ill-will was nothing compared with the violent anti-semitism from which they were flee-

---

6. For a sociological analysis of the classic concert as an elite ritual, see Small, C. (1987) 'Performance as ritual: sketch for an enquiry into the true nature of a symphony concert' in A.L. White (ed), *Lost In Music*. London: Routledge.

ing. On the other hand, there was the good fortune: the immigrants arrived just at the time when new economic possibilities were opening up.

The Jewish immigrants might have landed penniless in the New World. They might have been kept out of established professions and businesses. Yet this made them all the more ready to plunge into the new opportunities that the establishment considered beneath their dignity. Nowhere was this more true than in the entertainment industry.

Scientific inventions were creating the opportunity for new types of fortune-making. With the moving picture camera and the phonograph came the possibility of new entertainments for the working classes. If popular films and records could be produced, then sold on a massive scale, then there were fortunes to be made. By and large, respectable Protestant businessmen did not wish to demean themselves with these activities. At best they would have preferred to educate or preach to the masses, rather than amuse them with trivialities. By contrast, immigrant Jews were not slow to see the commercial opportunities in entertaining people just like themselves.

The New York music publishing companies which were established in the early years of the twentieth century, were largely the creation of Jews. The names of the major founders tell their own story: Maurice Shapiro, Louis Bernstein, Leo Feist, Isidore Witmark, Joseph Stern.[7] Some of the publishers were themselves composers and performers, such as the Witmark brothers, who played, with varied success, in vaudeville. For others, selling music was just another way of earning a living. Leo Feist, for instance, shifted his skills from selling corsets to selling sheet-music.[8]

7. Jasen, D.A. (1988) *Tin Pan Alley*. London: Omnibus.
8. Furia, P. (1992) *The Poets of Tin Pan Alley: the history of America's great lyricists*. New York: Oxford University Press, p21

To sell sheet-music, the publishers had to sign up song-writers who could turn out the music that the masses wanted to hear. Above all, the publishers were recruiting aspiring Jewish songwriters, who were steeped in the heritage of Yiddish songs and the music of the synagogue. Irving Berlin, for instance, was the classic immigrant composer. He arrived in the US as a four-year-old, with the name Israel Baline. His father had been a traditional cantor in Russia who, in the new world, had to earn his living by working in a kosher meat factory. Berlin may have written his earliest songs in Yiddish, but he knew, as he approached Tin Pan Alley publishers while still in his teens, that he would have to write in English if he were to capture the wider market. It was the same for other fledgling composers. Sammy Cahn, another of the great songwriters of the thirties, began his musical education by playing Yiddish songs on the piano for his mother. Professionally his songs would be in English.[9]

Just as the movie moguls were determined that their films would be American, and not overtly Jewish, so the songwriters wanted to prove that they belonged to this new land, including its Christian culture. Irving Berlin's songs celebrated 'White Christmas', rather than Chanukah, and 'Easter Parade' but not Passover. On the other hand, the Jewish Christmas songs were not ostensibly Christian in a religious sense. Berlin celebrates a secular Christmas of snow and log-fires; he does not mention anything about a divine birthday. Berlin's Easter is about bonnets, not crucifixion. He was paving the way for a non-theological Christianity, whose festivals could be promoted as national celebrations. Certainly, Berlin was proud to be an American, writing patriotic songs, including the 'unofficial' national anthem of the land to which his parents had brought him — 'God Bless America'.

---

9. Freedland, M. (1984) *So Let's Hear The Applause: the story of the Jewish entertainer*. London: Valentine Mitchell, p24.

The extent of the Jewish influence on American popular music before the age of rock is seen clearly in the musical. This American art form attracted the attention of the greatest songwriters of the pre-rock era: Jerome Kern, George and Ira Gershwin, Oscar Hammerstein, Richard Rogers, Lorenz Hart, Cole Porter, Alan Lerner and Frederick Loewe, not to mention Irving Berlin. Between them, they wrote the songs for practically all the great musicals of the thirties and forties. Nor should one forget Harold Arlen and Yip Harburg, who wrote the songs for the greatest of the screen musicals, *The Wizard of Oz*. With the exception of Cole Porter, all the above-named were Jewish. The tradition of the Jewish musical writer, in fact, continued into the rock era with Stephen Sondheim, Leonard Bernstein and Lionel Bart.

Cole Porter was aware that he was working in a medium that was disproportionately Jewish. He once told Richard Rogers that he had discovered the secret for writing hits: "I'll write Jewish tunes," he claimed.[10] Porter's comment was echoed by Jerome Kern, who, unlike Porter, was himself Jewish. Apparently, Oscar Hammerstein once asked what sort of music Kern would be writing for a stage musical about the life of Marco Polo. Kern replied: "It'll be good Jewish music".[11]

In one sense the music wasn't 'Jewish music' and Porter's tunes weren't 'Jewish tunes'. The Jewish composers were not simply adapting the Yiddish tunes of the ghetto for an English-speaking audience. They were drawing on the wider musical traditions of America. As Jeffrey Melnick has argued in his important book, *A Right To Sing The Blues*, the Jewish songwriters were, above all, adapting the music of African Americans.

---

10. Furia, *The Poets of Tin Pan Alley*, p155.
11. Melnick, J. (1999) *A Right To Sing The Blues: African Americans, Jews and American popular song*. Cambridge, Mass.: Harvard University Press, p79.

First, they took inspiration from ragtime music and, later, from jazz.[12]

Irving Berlin, in particular, was fascinated by the syncopated rhythms of ragtime. His first huge success was 'Alexander's Ragtime Band' in 1911, which, in fact, proved to be Tin Pan Alley's biggest hit up to that time. The previous year, Berlin had written 'Yiddle On Your Fiddle, Play Some Ragtime'. It had been a novelty number — an early song with essentially the same message as Chuck Berry's 'Roll Over Beethoven'. Move over, traditional music — something snappier is on the way. And the snappier stuff was coming from black music. Berlin's song, unlike Berry's, addressed a particular ethnic group: 'Yiddles' should start picking out the ragtime beat on their fiddles. The enormous success of 'Alexander's Ragtime Band', selling across ethnic divides, taught Berlin to address the whole of America, not just the Yiddles with their fiddles.

If Berlin borrowed African American rhythms and styles, then inevitably there were charges of plagiarism and exploitation. Scott Joplin, for one, thought that 'Alexander's Rag Time Band' had been based on his own work and he complained about receiving neither the recognition nor the financial remuneration.[13] It was even rumoured that Berlin kept 'a little coloured boy' in his basement to write his songs.[14] With charges of exploitation came those of debasement. Berlin and others, it was said, were sentimentalising ragtime, stripping it of its authenticity.

When, in the twenties and thirties, the craze for ragtime gave way to that for jazz, there were similar accusa-

---

12. Melnick argues that the music of African Americans was central to the success of Jews, whether as composers or performers: "The success of Jews was inseparable from their management of African American styles, resources and careers" (*A Right To Sing The Blues*, p31).
13. Melnick, p56.
14. Melnick, p115.

tions again. Al Jolson was the first big 'pop' star of the jazz age. He was the son of a cantor. His hit 'Swanee' was George Gershwin's first big success. The charges of sentimentalising and parodying African American music are easy to make in Jolson's case. Like many other Jewish vaudeville performers of that era, Jolson did not appear on stage as a Jew. He blacked up his face, playing in the tradition of minstrelsy singing ersatz 'minstrel' songs.[15]

Jolson's major film, the first 'singing talkie', was called 'The Jazz Singer'. Interestingly, in the film Jolson played a popular Jewish blackface singer, Jack Rubin, who became famous for his sentimental songs. Unusually, this film told a Jewish story. It portrayed the conflict between the old ways, depicted by Rubin's father, a traditional cantor, and the new ways of America, represented by Rubin's Christian girlfriend. The message was essentially assimilationist. Despite the film's success, it was a one-off: the major companies backed away from producing other obviously Jewish films.[16] The film's title showed how the word 'jazz' was becoming loosely used. It is highly debatable whether Jolson, or the character he played in the film, should properly be termed a 'jazz singer'.

Other Jewish composers and musicians, who had a deep-seated feel for jazz, would have certainly disputed Jolson's claims to be a jazz singer. Harold Arlen (né Hyman Arluck), to a much greater extent than Irving Berlin, respected the black musical traditions from which he was borrowing. Indeed, Arlen specifically took pride in writing for black jazz singers at Harlem's Cotton Club,

---

15. On the minstrel tradition, see Rogin, M. (1996) *Blackface, White Noise: Jewish immigrants in the Hollywood Melting pot.* Berkeley: University of California Press. In Britain the blackface television programme, *The Black and White Minstrel Show*, continued into the age of rock, only finishing in 1973. On the British blackface tradition, see Pickering, M. (1996) 'The BBC's Kentucky Minstrels, 1933-1950: blackface entertainment on British radio', *Historical Journal of Film, Radio and Television,* 16, 161-195; Pickering, M. (1997) 'John Bull in blackface', *Popular Music,* 16, 181-201.
16. Gabler, *An Empire Of Their Own,* pp. 140-146.

including most notably Cab Calloway. There were Jewish jazz musician-composers, like Benny Goodman, Mel Tormé and Artie Shaw, who played with black musicians and who consciously aimed to develop, not debase, jazz forms. They did not seek to transpose the complexities of jazz into catchy show tunes. Certainly, they did not appear on stage with blacked-up faces, repeating the parodied gestures of the stage 'coon'.[17]

Towering over all the other Jewish composers of Tin Pan Alley stands the figure of George Gershwin. Not only could he write a hit tune and turn out perfectly crafted songs for shows, but he wrote longer orchestrated pieces which bridged the gap between high and popular culture. He combined the traditions of European classical music with pop, jazz and blues. *Rhapsody In Blue* is a classic case in point. It is neither a symphony, nor is it jazz in a narrow sense. Nor is it an overture to a musical. It combines different musical forms to create something new.

In doing this, Gershwin was representing the position of the immigrant, wide-eyed and open-eared in the newly adopted land. As Jeffrey Melnick claims, it is no coincidence that it was a Jew who tried to forge unity from such musical diversity, in order to synthesise a new American music.[18] A Jew, such as Gershwin, did not want to remain stuck in the confines of tradition but was eager to embrace new musical influences. He had no hesitation — no restricting prejudices — against celebrating the art of black Americans. In fact, Gershwin grew up in Harlem and from an early age he was fascinated by the music he could hear on the streets. Later, with his brother Ira, George would visit the music cafés and get to know local

17. See, for instance, Collier, J. E. (1989) *Benny Goodman and the Swing Era*, New York: Oxford University Press; Firestone, R. (1993) *Swing, Swing, Swing: the life and times of Benny Goodman*, London: Hodder and Stoughton. Both books discuss whether Goodman took the initiative in integrating his band or whether he was reacting to the prompting of others.
18. Melnick, pp. 72ff.

black musicians and composers, such as Willie 'the Lion' Smith and James P. Johnson.[19]

In Gershwin's musical synthesis, Jewish music was not to the fore. Some claim that echoes of Klezmer music can be heard in the famous opening bars of *Rhapsody In Blue*. Tellingly, this echo is soon swamped in the main piece by modern rhythms. Gershwin had made plans to write a musical version of the old Yiddish folktale, *The Dybbuk*. Significantly, nothing came of this. *Porgy and Bess*, dealing with black characters in the Deep South, emerged instead.[20] George and Ira collaborated with DuBose Heyward to turn the latter's novel into a musical. Thankfully nothing came of an earlier plan to commission Hammerstein and Kern to write the score and then to use Al Jolson in the main role, complete with blackface.[21]

From the earliest performances, critics debated whether *Porgy and Bess* transposed African American music onto the New York stage, or whether the composer was using Broadway music to present African American characters. There is also the question whether the dialect of the lyrics ('dey' instead of 'they') reproduces or parodies black speech. For present purposes, it does not matter whether 'Summertime', 'It Ain't Necessarily So' and the rest of the tunes are to be classed as 'black' music or not.[22]

---

19. Singer, B. (1992) *Black and Blue: the life and lyrics of Andy Razaf*, New York: Schirmer, p141. Willie 'the Lion' Smith, in his turn, identified with Jews and possibly converted to Judaism - 'the Lion' of his nickname being a reference to the Lion of Judah.
20. Melnick, pp. 75f.
21. Furia, p141.
22. In the field of cultural studies, there has been debate whether it makes sense to talk of 'black' music. Some have criticised the notion that there are distinct musical traditions of black and white Americans. After all, even rural whites have sung their own versions of the blues, and blacks have incorporated European influences (see, for instance, Russell, T. *Blacks, Whites and Blues*. London: Studio Vista, 1970). On the other hand, Paul Gilroy has persuasively argued the 'anti anti-essentialist position', pointing out the absurdities of denying that there are cultural traditions (see, Gilroy, P. *The Black Atlantic*, Cambridge, Mass.: Harvard University Press, 1993).

Suffice to say, it is great music and it has moved black and white audiences through the years. The African American novelist, Maya Angelou, has described her emotions on seeing the black production of *Porgy and Bess*, which starred Cab Calloway. Even before the end of the first act she "had laughed, cried, exulted and mourned".[23] The second act, she writes, was even more moving.

There is no need to go into detail about the lives and careers of the great Jewish songwriters of the twenties and thirties. Others have told their story. However, the story of Tin Pan Alley needs to be mentioned in order to emphasise the extent of Jewish involvement in the musical tradition, against which rock seemed to be kicking. There is also another reason. Many aspects of the story of these earlier Jewish songwriters were to be reproduced later in the era of rock music.

We shall find Jewish composers of a later age drawn to the music of African Americans — this time to rhythm and blues, rather than to jazz or ragtime. There will be the debate whether white performers and composers were exploiting, even patronising, black music. Among the Jewish rock composers will be heirs of Gershwin, combining different elements of American music into new syntheses. There will be heirs of Harold Arlen, writing specifically for black singers and, in so doing, demonstrating their love for the African American musical heritage. Following Gershwin and the unrealised venture of *The Dybbuk*, we will see again inhibitions against expressing Jewish themes. And stepping into the footsteps of Berlin, Jewish composers of the rock era will write their Christmas songs.

All this will be found in the age of rock'n'roll — showing that rock did not mark the end of the story of the Jewish composer. Tin Pan Alley did not simply roll over like a timid animal, frightened by the sound of the electrified

23. Angelou, M. (1976) *Singin' and Swingin' and Gettin' Merry Like Christmas*. New York: Random House.

guitar. But not all is repetition. There was to be one significant difference between the age of rock and that of Tin Pan Alley's heyday. The Jewish performer was to become a rarity. Other ethnicities were to hold the rock stage, as Jews retreated backstage.

Music From The Margins

Popular music never keeps still. New and exciting trends inevitably become associated with a particular era. In their turn, they are condemned to appear old-fashioned in the eyes of the next generation. So it was with the traditions of Tin Pan Alley by the 1950s. Those children of Jewish immigrants had been so successful in moulding American popular culture that their music had become respectably mainstream. Once that happens to a popular musical tradition, it is time to move on.

Rock'n'roll arrived just as the older generation was trying to turn the clock back. Politically, the Eisenhower administration in the United States and the Conservative government in Britain were harking back to idealised, pre-war images of their respective countries. Young people, with money in their pockets, did not want to smooch to the music of their parents. They wanted something newer, more exciting, beyond conventional show-business and the decorous show tunes that were still coming out of Broadway. The so-called novelty tunes of those times were now distinctly not so novel. Many of the hits of the early fifties were still being written by Jews. Compositions by Dick Manning (né Samuel Medoff), such as 'Hot Diggity', 'Underneath The Linden Tree' and 'Takes Two To Tango', were typical of the cutesy hits of that time. Before he changed his name, Manning had hosted the radio show *Sam Medoff and his Yiddish Swing Orchestra*.

If the 'hot diggity' sounds that Tin Pan Alley was producing had seen better days, then one might expect that the new music would have different origins. The New York Jews had occupied centre stage in the thirties and forties; now, it would be time for others from the margins of society to sing in the spotlight of fame.[24]

Certainly rock'n'roll seemed to be coming from a very different source from the Tin Pan Alley. Robert Palmer succinctly sums it up in his book *Dancing in the Streets:* the new sounds of rock were "deeply rooted in nonmainstream cultures" and "existed on the margins of the pop-music business".[25] The early rock stars, such as Elvis, Jerry Lee Lewis and Gene Vincent, were, in the main, poor rural whites. A few blacks gained prominence, most notably Little Richard and Chuck Berry. All were men. Rock'n'roll, at least in its early days, projected an aggressive masculinity. And this was at variance with the softer — perhaps, more effeminate — traditions of Tin Pan Alley.

This, one might say, has become the 'official' history of rock. It is to be found in general encyclopedias. *Encarta*, possibly the most widely used encyclopedia in the world today, tells this story in its entry on Rock Music. Rock-'n'roll, it says, was "largely derived from the music of the American south" and this new music helped to "displace the New York City-based Tin Pan Alley songwriting tradition that had dominated the mainstream of American popular taste since the late 19th century".[26]

The Jewish dimension can easily be added into this 'official' story-line. Old Tin Pan Alley was full of big city Jews. The new music was coming from elsewhere. None of the early rock stars was Jewish. This would be entirely

---

24. This is the line taken by Melnick in *A Right To Sing The Blues*. Melnick concentrates on the relations between black and Jewish musicians in the pre-rock years. In a brief comment on rock, he implies that Elvis's arrival signalled the end of that relationship, for in the postwar years "Jews would be eclipsed by other white people who had different routes to Black sounds" (p203). He does not discuss the Jewish composers of the rock era.
25. Palmer, R. (1996) *Dancing in the Streets: a rock and roll history*, London: BBC Books, p16.
26. *Encarta 97 Encyclopedia*, Microsoft.

predictable if rock were the music of the poor southern margins. Therefore, it was 'thank you and good night' to the old Jewish tradition.

However, the public absence of Jews in rock'n'roll was not quite so simple. Jews were still in the background, playing significant roles. Alan Freed, a local disc jockey, became rock's "first super-promoter".[27] The story is that Freed's attention was first drawn to black music by his friend Leo Mintz, who owned a record shop in Cleveland and who told Freed about the obscure 'Race' records young whites were asking for.[28]

Freed started playing this 'Race' music on his radio programme. Basically this music was black boogie-woogie, or rhythm and blues, often played by southerners who had moved northwards to cities such as Chicago. They adapted the traditional blues format to a dance beat and electrified guitars. The early black rhythm and blues artists tended to record on small, independent labels, aimed at a black market. With Freed's backing this music started reaching a wider, interracial market. As the music grew in popularity, Freed started to organize live concert shows. One feature of these shows, that shocked civic dignitaries, especially in the South, was that they were interracial.

Many of the independent 'Race' labels were owned by Jews, who were operating independently of the established companies. Most notably there was Chess Records, owned by Leonard and Phil Chess, who had been born in Poland. Chess's catalogue includes classic recordings by Chuck Berry, Bo Diddley and Muddy Waters. Other owners of black labels were Syd Nathan (King Records), Herman Lubinsky (Savoy), Ike and Bess Berman (Apollo), and Ed and Leo Mesner (Philco-Aladdin). Atlantic Records, which, unlike the others, was to grow into a major com-

27. Szatmary, D.P. (1996) *A Time to Rock: a social history of rock-and-roll,* New Jersey: Prentice Hall p20.
28. Gillett, C. (1996) *The Sound of the City: the rise of rock & roll,* London: Souvenir Press, p13.

pany, was founded by a Jew, Herb Abramson, and a Turk, Ahmet Ertegun.

Nelson George, in his book *The Death of Rhythm & Blues*, offers an explanation as to why so many of such small recording companies were owned by Jews. He points out that blacks were not the only ones who suffered discrimination by the American business mainstream: "Unwelcome on Wall Street, many Jewish businessmen looked for places where there were fewer barriers to entrepreneurship".[29] Unlike mainstream white businessmen, whose lack of imagination or fastidious prejudices kept them from doing business with black producers and customers, these Jews dealt successfully in this corner of the market.

Some of the independent owners were undoubtedly disreputable, exploiting the black musicians whom they recorded and managed. Among the worst was Morris Levy, the owner of Roulette Records. He boasted of his mafia connections and he certainly did not pay black artists all they deserved. None of this prevented the Music Division of the United Jewish Appeal from honouring Levy as 'Man of the Year'.[30] However, as Nelson George makes clear, the few black owners of independent recording companies were themselves no gentle saints. Don Robey, for one, stands comparison with the roughest, most exploitative of the Jewish owners.[31] But not all was simple exploitation. Some of the Jewish owners, like the Chess brothers, had a genuine respect for the music that they were recording.

The small labels had a limited market, at least before Freed started publicising 'rock'n'roll'. Their records were played on black radio stations, which sprung up in the immediate post-war years. Their principal customers were black. They had little chance of breaking into the lucrative

---

29. George, N. (1988) *The Death of Rhythm & Blues*. London: Omnibus Press, p28.
30. Picardie, J. and Wade, D. (1993) *Atlantic and the Godfathers of Rock and Soul*. London: Fourth Estate.
31. George, *The Death of Rhythm and Blues*, pp. 31ff.

white market. In the early days of rock, it was taken for granted that any huge mega-star, capable of attracting a mass audience, would be White Anglo-Saxon Protestant.

Sam Phillips of Sun Records, who came from a typical poor Southern background, summed up the situation. He was famously quoted as saying "If I could find a white man who had the Negro sound and the Negro feel, I could make a billion dollars".[32] As all rock historians know, Phillips found such a man in Elvis. But Phillips failed to make his billion. After Elvis had cut a few records on Phillips' Sun label, he was lured to RCA, national success and the disastrous management of 'Colonel' Parker. Phillips received around $35,000 in compensation.[33]

More than any other rock star, Elvis Presley defined the new music. In the words of Greil Marcus, Elvis was "a supreme figure in American life, one whose presence no matter how banal or predictable, brooks no real comparison".[34] Elvis, himself, represented the new synthesis of country music and blues. He was a poor, white Southern boy, who grew up most definitely on the wrong side of the economic tracks. He was born in a two room log cabin. When he wandered into Sam Phillips's recording studios in Memphis as a shy teenager, he was working as a truck-driver. Country music was his heritage and his earliest recordings with Phillips reflected his country roots. He sang 'Blue Moon Of Kentucky', written by the blue-grass singer, Bill Monroe. But he didn't sing it in the style or tempo that Monroe had envisaged.

The young Elvis, like many other teenagers, had been listening to 'Race' music. Social life was as rigidly segregated as it had ever been, especially in the Deep South.

32. Friedlander, P. (1996) *Rock & Roll: a social history*, Boulder, CO: Westview Press, p44.
33. Escott, C. and Hawkins, M. (1992) *Good Rockin' Tonight: Sun Records and the birth of rock'n'roll*. London: Virgin.
34. Marcus, G. (1991) *Mystery Train: images of America in rock'n'roll music*. Harmondsworth: Penguin.

Elvis mixed with poor whites like himself, although he was a bit of a loner. He certainly did not have an African American social circle. The portable radio, however, was allowing a revolution in taste to occur. Alone in their bedrooms, away from parental supervision, white youngsters like Elvis were crossing the cultural lines of apartheid. By tuning into black radio stations, they could hear the latest sounds from Chicago. Elvis was to imitate the vocal styles of the black artists he heard, as were other early white rockers from the south. At the same time, across the racial divide, Chuck Berry was listening to country music stations — he knew where the big money lay.[35]

There has been much debate as to whether Elvis, and other white rock stars, created anything original or whether they stole black sounds and adulterated them, as Al Jolson might have done years before. Greil Marcus, for example, takes the line that Elvis was creating a style of singing that was different. The black music critic, Nelson George, puts the other side. Presley, he suggests, was only copying black rhythm & blues and he was "a mediocre interpretative artist" at that.[36] An academic sociologist, writing on rock's history, has suggested that the early white rock stars copied "Afro-American music with all its characteristic features, including the performance style of black musicians".[37] But, as will be seen, it's not just a matter of black and white. The ethnicity of Tin Pan Alley still had a part to play, right at the centre of rock'n'roll.

The new music attracted howls of protest, as well as screams of delight. When Elvis appeared on the Ed Sullivan Show, he was filmed from the waist up, lest the young audience be corrupted by his obscene hip movements. As always in American culture, race was never far from the surface. To the conventional guardians of white morality,

35. Berry, C. (1987) *The Autobiography*. London: Faber and Faber.
36. George, *The Death of Rhythm & Blues*, p63.
37. Wicke, P. (1990) *Rock Music: culture aesthetics and sociology*, Cambridge: Cambridge University Press, p16.

rock was dangerous because it seemed black, not that this could be said too directly in the post-war climate. In the US, various church authorities, especially in the south, complained about the dangers of the new 'jungle music'. 'Jungle' was a code-name for black.[38] The barbarians were not merely at the gates but in the home, on the radios and gramophones. Of course, previous generations of moral guardians had, in their own time, condemned the music of ragtime and jazz in much the same terms.

Part of the problem was sex. White fathers in the 1950s were proud to have bought refrigerators for the kitchen and televisions for the living-room. They also acquired radios for their children. They were shocked to discover that their daughters would use these symbols of affluence to lie on their beds, listening to men suggestively singing about sex. A white man, wriggling his hips and singing provocatively, was bad enough. But a black man doing the same would have been too much for white morality. Little Richard, with his effeminate gestures and make-up, was acceptable as a jokey figure (and marvellous singer). His stage name played down the danger. A Big Richard, playing it for real, would have been altogether too provocative for those days. As, indeed, was Chuck Berry, the one undoubted musical genius among those early rock performers. Berry's career was to grind to a halt following rather dubious charges of statutory rape. Yet, even the exuberance of Little Richard was a little too much for white middle-America. Each Little Richard record would be covered by blander singers, such as Pat Boone, whose pale skin and wholesome Christian background made for good royalty payouts.

---

38. For discussions of the rhetoric of rock's critics, see: Frith, C. (1996) *Performing Rites: on the value of popular music*, Oxford: Oxford University Press; Grossberg, L. (1993) 'The framing of rock: rock and the new conservatism', in *Rock and Popular Music*, ed. T. Bennett, S. Frith, L. Grossberg, J. Shepherd and G. Turner. London: Routledge. On the reception of rock in Britain, see: Chambers, I. (1985) *Urban Rhythms: pop music and popular culture*. London: Macmillan.

Thus, the story of these first generation rock stars seems to leave little room for Jews (nor did it leave much space for women performers). It is a story of poor black and white men, singing a direct, aggressive and masculine music. Or so the image indicates.

In a world of images, stereotypes are all important. The stereotype of Jews would seem to clash with the image of the male rocker. At that time, in the mid-fifties, there were male Jewish Hollywood stars. Nevertheless, the Kirk Douglas's and Tony Curtis's had to change their names, disguise their accents and avoid any Jewish parts. They had to pass publicly for non-Jews. We have to wait a couple of decades for the emergence of an openly Jewish male movie star. If today someone is asked to name a male Jewish film-actor, the odds would be short on their coming up with Woody Allen. Significantly, Woody Allen possesses those stereotypical features which make him unsuited for being an early rock'n'roller. He is small, weedy, short-sighted, verbally over-intellectual and seemingly ill-at-ease with his body: he's the eternal worrier, unable to allow himself a moment of relaxed fun without further worry. He's hardly a very masculine male. Just imagine Woody Allen, or anyone like him, in gold-lamé suit, singing 'Hound Dog' with a Presley leer and wiggle. The very image is laughable.

After the first wave of rock stars from the south came a number of softer, urban Italian stars. To achieve success, adjustments had to be made to their names. Tell-tale final vowels had to be dropped. Dion DiMucci was known as plain Dion. Freddy Picariello's surname was changed to Cannon. Fabian, who had been selected for stardom on the basis of his face, and certainly not for his voice, started life as Fabiano Forte Bonaparte. Overt signs of any ethnicity, other than WASPishness, were considered to be barriers to success.

There was one significant Jewish performer among the wave of softer singers coming just after that first generation of aggressive rockers. From 1959, Neil Sedaka had a series of hit singles: 'Oh! Carol', 'Happy Birthday Sweet Sixteen', 'Breaking Up Is Hard To Do', all of which Sedaka wrote or co-wrote.[39] In this case, the Jewish exception, by its exceptionality, confirms the gentile rule. Significantly, Sedaka was no sex-idol or macho-threat. He was baby-faced, with a hint of plumpness, singing in a pure, high-pitched of voice, which sounded as if it might not have broken yet. He looked like a good boy and was a concert-trained pianist, having attended the Juillard School of Music in New York. When he played the piano he played properly, behaving himself, unlike Jerry Lee Lewis, who thumped the keys and jumped on the lid. Sedaka's songs expressed a naive, almost asexual innocence. One of his earliest songs was 'I Go Ape'. The idea of Sedaka going ape does not conjure images of trashed hotels or empty cases of vodka: one might imagine a slightly untidy bedroom or a refusal to eat up breakfast cereal.

'Happy Birthday Sweet Sixteen', one of Sedaka's biggest hits, tells of a boy waiting for a girl's sixteenth birthday, when she would no longer be a child. If Presley had sung the song — or, worse still, if Chuck Berry had done so — it would have sounded disturbing, with suggestions of voyeurism, seduction and even abuse. In Sedaka's high-pitched voice, it just sounds charmingly naive: the sort of song mothers could play at their daughter's birthday parties. If exceptions prove rules, then the case of Sedaka emphasises, rather than contradicts, the contrast between the stereotypes of the rock'n'roller and the nice Jewish boy.[40]

Significantly, no Jewish boy achieved rock stardom in

---

39. Sedaka's song-writing will be discussed in Chapter Five.
40. In Britain, there was another exception during rock's first decade. Helen Shapiro had a period of brief fame without changing her name. As a schoolgirl, she was more a novelty figure than a serious rock-'n'roller. It was as if people were saying 'isn't it amazing that a young Jewish girl can sing with such a deep voice'. Her fame did not last. In later years, she became an Evangelical Christian.

the hand-picked way that Fabian did. Many of the rock promoters in the early days were Jewish.[41] In Britain, Larry Parnes, for example, kept a whole stable of domestic rockers, such as Billy Fury, Marty Wilde, Terry Dene and Dickie Pride. Parnes was to have much cause for regret in passing up an opportunity to sign the Beatles. When Parnes went looking for potential stars, he did not start with his own community. He was principally looking at non-Jewish young men, as were so many other Jewish managers of that time.

Certainly, an overtly Jewish name would have been unsuitable for a rock singer in those days. Even today, the idea of a rock star called Irving Weinberg or Harvey Goldstein seems absurd. But why is the very idea so humorous? The joke, of course, depends on a clash of stereotypes. Jerry Lee Lewis fits the image. But Jerry Lee Levy must be a parody — the Jew in an inappropriate place.

* * *

By a selective gathering of facts and stereotypes, it is possible to construct a predictable picture. On the rock stage, we have WASPs, a few blacks and some Italians, equipped with non-Italianate names. Rocking Jews are hard to find. Off-stage, there are Jews aplenty. Thus, it would seem that the torch of creativity had passed from the Jews,

---

41. Rogan, J. (1988) *Starmakers and Svengalis: the history of British pop management*. London: Queen Anne Press. Rogan, in the final chapter of his book, asks why so many managers were Jewish (and homosexual). He offers no fully convincing explanation, except to point to the continuing high level of anti-semitism in fifties Britain. It is easy to forget, he writes, that "blatantly racist epithets such as 'jew boy' and 'yid' were common expressions during that time, in the same way that 'paki shop' can today be heard in polite middle-class homes without causing comment" (p277). But that is no explanation in itself, unless coupled with an account that shows how Jewish entrepreneurs, like Asian entrepreneurs today, were drawn to unconventional businesses, where they could build up their own networks of contact.

whose 'Jewish tunes' dominated American popular music in the twenties and thirties. Something more virile was required for the music of the fifties. It was time for the margins to enter centre stage.

To be sure, Jewish entertainers continued in the glitzier, kitschier ends of show-business, even recording the occasional rock-type song. Interestingly, the more obviously Jewish a performer appeared, the more the image was of show-bizz, 'all-round entertainers' and an earlier, tuxedoed era, rather than of rock. In the United States, Steve Lawrence (who, in good traditional style, was the son of a cantor) and Edie Gormé survived the rock onslaught, but no-one ever confused them for rock stars. Nor did Barbra Streisand take the rock path. Barry Manilow, at ease with tux, bow-tie and big band, also evokes an earlier era. In Britain, Frankie Vaughan (né Abelson) had a string of hits. With his cane and high-kicking routine, he was 'Mr Entertainment', uncool and delightfully dated in the age of rock.

Perhaps the move away from the 'Jewish tunes' of the older generation is aptly illustrated by a very minor figure in the history of British pop. In the early fifties, Robert Earl had several hits with big, sentimental ballads. After the arrival of rock, a singer like Earl became immediately old-fashioned. In subsequent years, he deliberately played to a small, ageing Jewish audience, recording Yiddish favourites such as 'Mom-e-le'. His son, also called Robert, entered show-business, but on the management side. He now heads the Hard Rock Café chain and is apparently listed as one of the UK's hundred richest people.[42] There, in the story of one show business dynasty, seems to be written a wider pattern of sociological change.

Yet, there's something missing. Under the influence of stereotypes we tend to notice only some facts, mistaking

42. Larkin, C. (1997) *The Virgin Encyclopedia of Sixties Music*. London: Virgin.

the part for the whole. We see non-Jewish rockers, uncool Jewish performers, and hear about the back-stage deals of Jewish managers. That seems enough to complete the picture.

But there is something more. Who wrote the words and music that flowed so wonderfully from the mouths of the visible singers? Who created the new sounds in the studios? Other work was being done, away from the public gaze. And the older traditions of Gershwin, Arlen and Berlin had not necessarily rolled over in defeat.

Writing For Elvis: Leiber and Stoller

Elvis Presley is the great icon of rock'n'roll. Even now, more than twenty years after his death, Elvis's image is instantly recognizable. This in itself says something important about the age of rock-'n'roll. During the Tin Pan Alley era, the composers, such as Irving Berlin, Cole Porter and George Gershwin were household names. In the age of rock, by contrast, the performer is everything. Elvis, with his looks, his smile and, above all, his voice, swamped his material. When he sung, rock'n'roll seemed so direct — so different from the artificiality of show-bizz type music. It was easy to think that the words and music were coming directly from Elvis's soul, without the intermediary of any third parties.

Yet this was an illusion. Presley, apart from a few exceptions, did not write his own songs. His performance depended on earlier acts of creation. In this new age, when the public were buying records, rather than sheet-music, it was the singer's name, not the writer's, that was the attraction. Management had a vested interest in keeping the writers out of the limelight. They did not want it known that this new, vital music might have been written by older men or by uncharismatic geeks. The star, suitably macho and anglo, had to stand alone. Composers were dimmed to the point of invisibility by the star's brilliance.

Years later, Bob Dylan described the impact of first hearing Elvis's 'Hound Dog' in 1956. Like all fans, the young Dylan wanted to believe that there was nothing between Presley and his music. In an interview, Dylan said that it was 'Hound Dog' that first got him into rock, when he was still at school. It was the performance that was overwhelming: "It didn't matter who wrote it... It was just there".[1]

Elvis Presley's record 'Hound Dog' was like an explosion, announcing that rock'n'roll was here to stay. It was not the first rock record to make a national impact. Elvis, earlier that year, had his first US number one with 'Heartbreak Hotel', a slower, intense song. 'Hound Dog', with its machine-gun drum roll, moved and jumped with an energy unlike almost any other record that had previously entered the US or British hit parades. The US B-side was 'Don't Be Cruel'. The record stayed at the top of the US charts for an amazing eleven weeks. To this day, no record has occupied the number one spot for longer in the United States.

But 'Hound Dog' wasn't 'just there', whatever young fans like Dylan might have assumed. Like any song, it had to be written. The song has an interesting story, which tends to be left untold by the popular histories of rock, which fill their pages with glossy pictures of the performers.[2] Even academic histories often tell only half the story. This is particularly true of those books which wish to argue that white rocks stars, such as Presley, appropriated authentic black music. If all is subsumed to a simple matrix of black-white relations, then the Jewish dimension gets lost. It is a crucial dimension: 'Hound Dog', that great emblem of the classic rock'n'roll song, had Jewish authors. And so did many more of Presley's famous songs.

The History of 'Hound Dog'

At first glance, the story of 'Hound Dog' seems a classic example of what has been called the "blanching of

---

1. Zollo, P. (1997) *Songwriters on Songwriting: expanded edition*. New York: Da Capo Press, p83.
2. For an example, see McCarthy, D. (1990) *The Golden Age of Rock*. London: Apple Press.

rock".[3] A white artist copies a black one and then takes all the glory, not to mention financial rewards. The black artist remains in obscurity and hardly anyone realises that the famous white singer has plagiarised a black one.

White teenagers, such as the young Bob Dylan, hearing 'Hound Dog' for the first time, would not have known that there had been a previous version. Three years earlier, the song had been recorded by the black singer Willie Mae (Big Mama) Thornton on the small, independent Peacock label. It was played exclusively on the black radio stations and had been a hit on the R&B ('black') charts. In fact, Willie Mae's version had been number one for seven weeks in 1953. Her success had not impinged on the white market.

Sam Phillips, always on the look-out for the main chance, quickly wrote an answer-song to 'Hound Dog'. He rushed Rufus Thomas into the studio to record 'Bear Cat'. The tunes were identical, and so were some of the lines. But the gender of the song had been altered. Willie Mae had been bemoaning that her man was nothing but a hound dog. Rufus Thomas complained that his woman was nothing but a bear cat. Rufus's version, addressed to the female cat, also sold well in the black market, going to number 3 in the R&B charts. Sam Phillips was later to be successfully sued for plagiarism. He readily admitted that he stole the tune and many of the words.[4]

Curiously, when Elvis recorded the song, he used the original version. Although early rock often expressed an aggressive masculinity, on this most famous of all records, Elvis was ostensibly singing to a man — to the hound dog. However, the lyrics were changed. He could not repeat Willie Mae's version, the words of which had been specifically written for a woman to sing, berating her selfish, exploitative man. You ain't looking for a woman, Willie

---

3. Szatmary, D. (1987) *A Time To Rock: a social history of rock'n'roll.* New York: Schirmer Books, pp. 27ff.
4. Escott, C. and Hawkins, M. (1992) *Good Rockin' Tonight: Sun Records and the birth of rock'n'roll*, London: Virgin, p40.

Mae had complained, you're just looking for a home. There was sexual innuendo, playing on the hound theme: you can wag your tail, she sang, but you're not going to get fed. She hinted that maybe she was, despite all her complaints, caught by desire: you make me moan and cry.

Lyrically, Elvis's version is far inferior. The subtlety and irony were lost. So were most of the original words. Something obscure about never catching a rabbit was added. The one rhyme in Elvis's version is not true ('mine'/'time'). Yet, these losses cannot be put down to a white misappropriating, and then watering down, black art. Nor is it that a male singer has coarsened the sensitive words of a woman. The original words and music were written by two young Jewish males: Jerry Leiber and Mike Stoller. Jerry Leiber, the lyricist, was later to make little secret of his preference for the Willie Mae version.[5]

The background of 'Hound Dog' is worth mentioning because it would be so easy to assume that Presley was merely 'blanching' Willie Mae's music. Certainly, some academics who wish to tell the story of whites appropriating black music, use 'Hound Dog' as an example. But, in doing so, they only tell half the story.

Peter Wicke, the head of the Centre for Popular Music Research at Humboldt University in Berlin, is the author of *Rock Music*.[6] This sociological study has been well received in academic circles, particularly in the field of cultural studies. Wicke argues that rock'n'roll was based on white singers stealing "black music". According to Professor Wicke, "the great successes of rock often turn out on closer inspection to be white cover versions of Afro-

---

5. Guralnick, P. (1994) *Last Train to Memphis: the rise of Elvis Presley.* Boston: Little, Brown, p406. In fact, Leiber and Stoller had to go to court to have their authorship of the original Willie Mae version confirmed. The white rhythm and blues band-leader, Johnny Otis, had managed to have his name inserted as an author (Escott and Hawkins, *Good Rockin' Tonight*).
6. Wicke, P. (1990) *Rock Music: culture, aesthetics and sociology.* Cambridge: Cambridge University Press.

American blues and rhythm & blues songs". He offers a familiar example: "Even the song that gave Elvis Presley his commercial breakthrough in 1956, 'Hound Dog', had already been released three years earlier by the blues singer Willie Mae Thornton".[7] All very true as far as it goes. But it doesn't go quite far enough. Wicke does not mention the songwriters, nor their ethnicity.

Deena Weinstein, an American professor of cultural sociology, also writes of the white appropriation of black music. She discusses four white cover versions of early black rock records, including Presley's cover of Thornton.[8] In each case, she points out that the white artist, aiming at a "wider and whiter audience", gained the profits denied to the black artist. She mentions that Elvis built his career on cover versions. In discussing how white performers copied black artists, she concentrates on the singers. She does not mention the composers, including the composers of 'Hound Dog'.

A final example can be offered to show that, even when song-writing is considered, assumptions can still lead experts in the wrong direction. Philip Ennis's *The Seventh Stream* is a serious, well-researched book on the history of rock. In talking of the development of black music, he discusses how the oral tradition, by which songs were passed down from mouth to mouth, was transformed into a written tradition. As black music became popularized, so the songs were written down and then copyrighted by music publishers. He offers the example of Willie Mae Thornton's 'Hound Dog'. Its lyrics were particularly strong, he says, and the song "represented a credible member of an accepted black song style and it was written". He comments further that "the authors were part of the growing development in black pop wherein the written song and

---

7. Wicke, p39.
8. Weinstein, D. (1998) 'The history of rock's pasts through rock covers' in *Mapping the Beat: popular music and contemporary theory*, ed. T. Swiss, J. Sloop and A. Herman. Oxford: Blackwell.

arrangements were supplanting the older oral tradition".[9] Thus, Ennis conveys the impression that the authors of 'Hound Dog' belonged to a black tradition of music. He does not discuss how it could have happened that this 'credible' piece of black music had Jewish composers.

'Hound Dog' was not a one-off. So many of Elvis's big hits had Jewish authors. Of course, he sang songs by black composers. For instance, Otis Blackwell wrote 'All Shook Up', 'Return to Sender' and 'Paralyzed', as well as 'Don't Be Cruel', the flip-side of 'Hound Dog'. Arthur Crudup wrote 'That's All Right' and 'My Baby Left Me', which Elvis had recorded on Sun Records, before his big commercial break-through. Not unusually for a black composer, Crudup failed to receive due royalties for his songs. Hill and Range, Presley's publishers, refused to pay back royalties. Crudup died in poverty in the early seventies.[10]

More of Elvis's famous hits were composed by Jews than by blacks. In addition to 'Hound Dog', the team of Leiber and Stoller wrote 'Don't', 'Jailhouse Rock', 'King Creole', 'I Want To Be Free', 'Baby I Don't Care', and 'Treat Me Nice'. Aaron Schroeder, with a variety of partners, contributed 'Stuck On You', 'Good Luck Charm', 'Big Hunk O'Love', 'Any Way That You Want Me', 'I Got Stung' and 'Got A Lot Of Living To Do'. Schroeder also wrote the English version of 'It's Now Or Never', which was originally an Italian ballad and which became Elvis's first massive hit after leaving the army in 1960. Doc Pomus, mostly in collaboration with Mort Shuman, contributed another raft of classic Elvis songs: 'Little Sister', 'His Latest Flame', 'A Mess Of Blues', 'She's Not You' (with Leiber and Stoller), 'Surrender', 'Viva Las Vegas' and 'Suspicion'. Doc Pomus's great contribution to rock and to rhythm and blues will be discussed separately in the

---

9. Ennis, P.H. (1992) *The Seventh Stream: the emergence of rock'n'roll in American popular music*. Hanover: University Press of New England, p194, (emphasis in original).
10. Szatmary, *A Time To Rock*, p66.

following chapter. The 'Jewish' list thus contains a fair measure of Elvis's rocking hits, as well as his softer ballads.

In short, Elvis may have represented the rebellious margins of society, rebelling against the orthodoxies of conventional popular music. But, sociologically speaking, much of his music was coming from the same source, one generation removed, as the classic music of Tin Pan Alley. It was still urban Jews who were writing hit songs. Like the great Jewish composers of Tin Pan Alley before them, they were drawing on the latest developments in African American music to do so. This substantial Jewish contribution was hidden by the acceptably WASPish aura of the new, young mega-stars.

Leiber and Stoller

Jerry Leiber and Mike Stoller were still in their teens when they wrote 'Hound Dog'. Both were born in 1933, making them Elvis's senior by a year. Leiber was born in Baltimore, while Stoller was born in Belle Harbor, New York. Both families moved westwards to Los Angeles, where the two met at high school.[11]

Jerry Leiber's background was the poorer of the two. His father, who had emigrated from Poland, died when Jerry was five. With the insurance money, his mother opened a small grocery store in a none too affluent area of Baltimore. Jerry recalled later that she was one of the few shopkeepers in the area who would give credit to black customers. Jerry would help with the deliveries of coal and kerosene. He was regularly welcomed into the homes of the black customers. And there he would hear their radios, playing a type of music he had never heard before. He was

---

11. Much of the background information on Leiber and Stoller is taken from Robert Palmer's excellent *Baby That Was Rock & Roll: the legendary Leiber and Stoller*. New York: Harvest, 1978.

captivated: "Those radios were like magic boxes to me", he was to recall.[12]

Jerry was clearly something of a wayward, street-wise kid. He was always hanging out with the sort of boys whom his uncles disapproved of. One of his uncles had tried to encourage him to attend the Jewish youth group, Habonim. It wasn't for Jerry. He recalled that it was "a bunch of ugly girls and fat boys holding hands and dancing the *hora*".[13] The comment is revealing. The Jewish group, and its music, is dismissed as uncool. Jerry was looking for sharper company; that meant entering a wider world.

In 1945, Mrs Leiber sold up the shop and took the family to California in a Greyhound bus. Their new home was near the film studios in Los Angeles. During his high school years, Jerry started writing songs, especially lyrics. He also took to visiting the film studios looking for work. The idea of becoming a professional songwriter was not outlandish. As happens again and again in the story of rock's Jewish songwriters, there were connections with the networks of Tin Pan Alley. In Leiber's case it was a family connection. His older sister had married the son of a songwriter, who also wrote scores for films. The songwriter was not a mythical figure, only to be read about in magazines. It was someone in the family.

At high school, Jerry was looking for a collaborator, who could set his lyrics to music. The name of Mike Stoller was suggested. The quiet and much more studious Stoller was at first sceptical, wary of the more outgoing Leiber. Indeed, Mike suspected that Jerry would want him to write conventional, slushy pop songs. However, they soon realized their common interest in blues and boogie.

Mike's family background was more economically secure than Jerry's. His father, after a series of jobs, had

---

12. Palmer, p12.
13. Palmer, p15.

built up a business for contracting machine tools. Again, there was a family connection with Tin Pan Alley. Mike's mother had been an actress, appearing on Broadway in the chorus of George Gershwin's musical *Funny Face*. She encouraged Mike to study piano. Above the Stollers' piano in their apartment living-room, was a signed photograph of Gershwin at his piano. The image of Gershwin, hanging over Mike as he practised, contained an important message: a Jewish boy, who worked hard at his music, could succeed like the great Gershwin.

The Stollers lived in a neighbourhood which had a large Mexican-American population. Mike listened to the Latin music of his neighbours and, in fact, joined a Pachuco social club.[14] This mix of black boogie, Latin rhythms and old Tin Pan Alley craft would be crucial in the music of Leiber and Stoller. Again, there is an echo of the earlier Jewish popular composers, such as Gershwin. They, too, had grown up in city neighbourhoods, where, down the streets, they would hear the music of other ethnic groups; later they would incorporate these rhythms and sounds into their works.[15] Something more exciting than their own Jewish musical tradition always seemed to be beckoning — Latino or African American dancing would appear more exotic than the boring old *hora*.

The position of the lower-middle-class store-keeper has historically been a fragile one. One bad break — a batch of non-paying customers and unreliable suppliers, or the opening of a better financed rival concern — and the small business can collapse, with the family rejoining the ranks of the poor. Many who have occupied the precarious position of the lower-middle-class look up with admiration at the social world above them. No doubt some of Leiber and Stoller's Jewish class mates at Fairfax High School aspired to the golf clubs and elite colleges which still excluded

---

14. Palmer, p16.
15. See Melnick, *A Right To Sing The Blues*, pp. 52f.

Jews. Others in the lower-middle class have looked with admiration, and even with a touch of envy, in the opposite social direction. They have seen energy, warmth and humanity in the lives of those worse-off. This was the view of African Americans that Leiber communicated to Stoller.

Soon the pair were writing 'black songs' and dating black girls. Perhaps their families worried. However, Mike's mother would have known that her hero, too, had been drawn to the music of African Americans. There are signs of parental encouragement. George Gershwin, it is said, had a black piano teacher.[16] When Mike had started showing an interest in boogie-woogie, and had abandoned his classical lessons, his parents, on the recommendation of a neighbour, arranged for him to be taught by the great 'stride' pianist, James P. Johnson.[17] Not only had Johnson been an accomplished composer in his own right and a director of all-black Broadway reviews — he had also been a personal friend of Gershwin. By the time he taught Mike Stoller, Johnson was very much a sick man in decline.[18]

Mike and Jerry, having connections with the Jewish world of song-writing, knew who to take their 'black' songs to. Through Lester Sill, a local manager for an independent label, they were able to bring their songs to the attention of the Robins, a black singing group. Sill arranged for them to have an audition with the Robins, and they sang their composition 'That's What The Good Book Says'. The audition was successful. The Robins recorded the song and Mike and Jerry began writing regularly for the group.

From this, Mike and Jerry graduated to writing for some of the best R&B singers of the time, such as LaVern Baker, Jimmie Witherspoon, Joe Turner and Amos Milburn. These singers are now recognized as being amongst

---

16. Melnick, p55.
17. Palmer, p16.
18. Johnson and Gershwin are discussed in Singer, B. (1992) *Black and Blue: the life and lyrics of Andy Razaf.* New York: Schirmer.

50

the precursors of rock'n'roll.[19] The Robins were recording
on the small label, Spark, which had limited distribution.
The music came to the attention of another independent
label, Atlantic, which was building its reputation in the
world of R&B. In 1956 Atlantic took over Spark, along
with the songwriting talents of Mike and Jerry. Some of
the Robins, however, did not want to transfer to the new
company. So the group split, with the lead singer and bass
singer going with Leiber and Stoller and reforming the
group as the Coasters.

Leiber and Stoller were not content merely to copy
black rhythm and blues, but they were developing their
own style as composers. Among Leiber and Stoller's early
works was 'Kansas City', which they originally entitled
'K.C. Loving'. The song became a 'black' hit for Wilbert
Harrison, and was later to be popularized world-wide by
the Beatles. For this song, Mike did not want to write a
standard blues arrangement, but he felt the words would
benefit from more melodic originality.[20] Was this a case of
'blanching' a pure African American medium, giving it a
pretty, 'white' show-bizzy twist? All that can be said is
that the song was to be recorded by black rhythm and
blues singers such as Muddy Waters, Hank Ballard, Memphis Slim, Jimmy Witherspoon, Little Milton, T-Bone
Walker, James Brown etc and etc. The list reads like a ver-
itable 'Who's Who' of great R&B artists. If they can't be
trusted to spot a good R&B song, then who can?

To write lyrics for black singers involved Leiber writing
in an idiom that was not exactly his own. He was like a
playwright creating dialogue for other characters. In one
obvious sense, the black world differed from his own. It
was a Christian world and its popular music, even its
dance music, was heavily influenced by the church and
gospel traditions. To write in this idiom would mean using

19. Tosches, N. (1991) *Unsung Heroes of Rock'n'Roll* London: Secker
    and Warburg.
20. Palmer, p19.

51

gentile points of reference. The first song which Leiber and Stoller sang for the Robins is a case in point, with its gospel references to 'the good book'.

Later Leiber and Stoller were to write 'Saved' for LaVerne Baker. The song tells of a woman who used to drink, smoke and gamble, but now her soul is saved for the kingdom to come. She declares herself to be part of the big, drum-beating soul-saving army. All the imagery is Christian. But the Jewish songwriters stop short of mentioning Jesus. They still keep their distance, just like Irving Berlin's 'White Christmas'. And, in their turn, Leiber and Stoller were not to shrink from writing the odd Christmas song. They wrote 'Santa Claus Is Back In Town' for Elvis.

This sense of familiarity, but apartness, is crucial for the work that Leiber and Stoller did first with the Robins, and later when the band was reconstituted as the Coasters. Their rock was highly verbal. It did not have the non-verbal excitement of Little Richard whose call 'Awopbopaloo bopalop bamboom' conveys an urgency beyond mere words. Leiber and Stoller described their songs as 'playlets'. They created characters and stories, commenting on the world about them. In the world of early rock'n'roll, only Chuck Berry also did this sort of thing.

The playlets were primarily written for black voices and used black slang. Yet, at the same time, they depicted universal themes of love, life and, above all, teenage insecurity. Leiber was not using the sort of stage black dialect that Ira Gershwin had employed in *Porgy and Bess*: Leiber did not substitute 'dat' and 'dey' for 'that' and 'they'. It was more a question of intonation and the occasional 'hip' word. Nevertheless, it was an important step. In a world dominated by white Anglo-Saxon images, black life was being presented as a mirror in which all teenagers could recognize themselves.

Leiber and Stoller were clearly on the side of mischief, fun and the insecure. 'Charlie Brown' tells of the big dope who always gets caught at school. Everyone else might run away from trouble, but Charlie Brown's gonna get caught, just you wait and see. The joke is that he sounds perplexed. The other voices in the band are gently mocking him. In 'Yakety Yak' we hear a teenager being told to do all the household tasks, before being allowed out at the weekend. You've got to bring in the dog and then put out the cat. The voice of parental authority goes 'yakety yak'.

'Along Came Jones' also uses dialogue between the lead singer and the rest of the Coasters. The singer tells of a western adventure programme he saw on television, on 'Channel Two' to be precise. The villain grabs the girl. And then? the others keep asking. He threatens her. He ties her up. And then? At the last moment, along comes the hero Jones, long lean lanky Jones, to make an improbable rescue. So the song spoofs the Western. It is possibly the first major pop song to take television as its topic. More than anything, it shows how Leiber and Stoller were not merely reproducing the music of others, but were observing the times and catching the social changes in their songs.

Sexual insecurities are portrayed with understanding humour. In 'Poison Ivy' the singers warn young boys not to get involved with girls. Otherwise you'll get an unscratchable itch, which will require an ocean of Calamine lotion. In 'Love Potion # 9' the singer admits to being a flop with girls. He consults a gypsy about his problem. She gives him a special potion. And now he's kissing everyone, including a cop.

Hit after hit followed for the Coasters and for other groups with whom Leiber and Stoller worked. These records sold hugely on both sides of America's racial divide. Robert Palmer in *Dancing in the Streets* rightly praises the "sophisticated and self-conscious artistry" of the songs Leiber and Stoller wrote for the Coasters. Palmer quotes Leiber half jokingly comparing his lyrics with the novels of William Styron and William

Faulkner.[21] Those two novelists required hundreds of pages to create their stories. Leiber and Stoller could present characters, tell tales and crack jokes inside a couple of verses, together with a chorus that sticks in the brain and a brief instrumental break. Not a second was wasted. 'Yakety Yak' said all that it needed to say in under two minutes (one minute, forty-three seconds, to be precise).

Leiber and Stoller were well aware that the new technology demanded a different approach to song-writing. What counted was the recording, not the written sheet-music. They used to say, in a much repeated phrase, that 'we write records, not songs'. In their composing, Leiber and Stoller envisaged the form and sound of the final record. Inevitably they became involved in the actual processes of recording. In fact, when they signed for Atlantic Records, they did so as independent producers, so that they could supervise the recording sessions.

Leiber and Stoller took minute care with the recording of the Coasters' records. In doing so, they were anticipating recording procedures that were to become standard practice. Their aim was to create the perfect performance in the studio, rather than capture the group's actual stage performances. They made take after take, splicing the recordings to achieve perfect timing for the delivery of the comic lines. While the practice was laboured, the aim was always to produce the effect of spontaneity. 'Yakety Yak' sounds fresh. It is as if the singers, the saxophone player and the other musicians, had just walked into the studio and the music had poured out in one happy burst. It wasn't so. Effort was required to produce the sounds of effortlessness.

Leiber and Stoller continued to develop new sounds, particularly in their work with another black singing group, that was to achieve even greater success than the Coasters.

---

21. Palmer, R. (1996) *Dancing in the Streets*, London: BBC Books, p39.

The Drifters had originally been formed in 1953, with Clyde McPhatter as the lead singer. With McPhatter's high, gospel-trained voice, the Drifters had a series of R&B hits, including, coincidentally, a re-working of Irving Berlin's old 'White Christmas'. However, McPhatter left for military service and in 1958 the group's manager, George Treadwell, sacked the remaining members of the band. Holding the copyright to the group's name, Treadwell simply recruited a new bunch of singers, with Ben E. King taking the lead, and then renamed them as the 'The Drifters'.[22]

Leiber and Stoller worked closely with these new Drifters. Their first record was extraordinary. The song 'There Goes My Baby', of which Leiber and Stoller were co-writers, did not follow the usual format of tightly structured and rhyming verses, followed by a clear, hummable chorus. One critic has described the song as being "virtually free form".[23] The production was also innovative. Instead of the usual solid R&B rhythm, Leiber and Stoller experimented with a broken, Latin rhythm, using Latin American percussion instruments. Orchestral strings were featured in the instrumental break, echoing classical motifs. Stoller described the strings as playing a "Rimsky-Korsakov-Borodin pseudo line".[24] Above this complex arrangement soared the soulful voice of Ben E. King. As Leiber was to say, "we were trying to create a collage".[25]

The resulting sound was very different from standard rock or rhythm and blues. When Jerry Wexler, the co-head

---

22. On the complex history of the Drifters, see B. Millar (1971) *The Drifters: the rise and fall of the black vocal group*. London: Studio Vista.
23. Gillett, C. (1996) *The Sound of the City: the rise of rock & roll*, London: Souvenir Press, p198.
24. Wexler, J. and Ritz, D. (1994) *Rhythm and the Blues*, London: Jonathan Cape, p136. Others have heard hints of Tchaikovsky. Bob Millar writes that the song might have been called 'There Goes Tchaikovsky' (*The Drifters*, p60).
25. Quoted in Millar, *The Drifters*, pp. 60-1.

of Atlantic Records and a great supporter of R&B, first heard the recording, he thought it an absolute mess. Jerry Leiber describes Wexler's reaction in graphic terms: "Jerry Wexler was eating his lunch on his desk and he said 'Man, get the fuck out of here with that'".[26] Wexler wrote in his autobiography that "to me it sounded like a radio caught between two stations". He pronounced it "dog-meat" and refused to release it for a year.[27] Eventually, Wexler relented. In April 1959 the record was released and went to number one in the US charts. Like the Coasters, the Drifters had broken out of the confines of the 'black' market.

Other Drifters records followed, also using strings and the South American rhythm known as 'baion'. They also achieved huge success in both the pop and R&B charts. Some of the songs were written by Leiber and Stoller, such as 'Dance With Me', while 'On Broadway' was co-written with Barry Mann and Cynthia Weil. For some of the records that they produced, Leiber and Stoller recruited other songwriters — again principally Jewish writers like themselves. Doc Pomus and Mort Shuman wrote 'Save The Last Dance For Me', one of the Drifters' greatest hits. On occasions, Burt Bacharach arranged the string section for Drifters' recordings. Bacharach also wrote 'Please Stay' for the group.

In 1960 Ben E. King split from the Drifters to pursue a solo career. The reason was financial. The Drifters were a hired band, firmly under the control of their manager, who paid them a fixed and none too generous salary. Conse-quently the singers were failing to profit from the massive sales of their records. King was thoroughly disenchanted with the set-up. Leiber and Stoller continued to work with him, producing his early solo records. They collaborated with King to write jointly, 'Stand By Me'. For 'Spanish

---

26. Millar, *The Drifters*, p60.
27. Wexler and Ritz, *Rhythm and the Blues*, p136.

Harlem', another large hit, Leiber combined with the young Phil Spector. Both records, like those of the Drifters, were successful with both black and white audiences.

By the time of King's 'Spanish Harlem', the combination of gospel tenor, Latin rhythm, electric guitar and orchestral strings no longer appeared a strange mishmash. The elements seemed perfectly at one with each other, as if the combination occurred naturally. But that is the genius of art: to take elements which seem totally discrepant and then to combine them in such a way that one cannot imagine how they could have once existed separately. It was a trick that Gershwin had pulled off triumphantly twenty-five years before the era of rock. Now, again, it was Jewish composers from the city creating through synthesising; seeing how European, African-American and Latin music could be united into something new.

In rock music, continual success cannot be guaranteed. Leiber and Stoller could not maintain their success throughout the sixties. As the civil rights movement developed and the opposition to the war in Vietnam became vocal, Leiber and Stoller had wanted to persuade the Coasters to record material with a harder edge of political protest. The group preferred to stay with the style that had brought them success in apparently more seemingly innocent times. But to stand still is to get left behind.

Increasingly, Leiber and Stoller were concerned with recording. In 1964 they established their own recording company, Red Bird. They sold Red Bird to their partner, George Goldner, an older New York Jew who had a chequered history producing black and Latin American records. The business side of things didn't particularly appeal to Leiber and Stoller. As Leiber said, "I'm not a businessman, I'm a songwriter".[28] The pair continued to work as independent record producers throughout the

28. Quoted in Millar, *The Drifters*, p100.

seventies and eighties. Their time of innovation, however, had passed.

A Moral Vision

The early critics of rock completely misunderstood the music. They heard the boogie beat and the sensuous singing. All they could hear was the collapse of morality and the dangerously encroaching sounds of 'the jungle'. But they did not listen. In the hands of Leiber and Stoller, this was not music to threaten the end of civilization. It was humane, inclusive music. If it threatened, then its targets were the forces of bigotry.

Symbolically, the music combined the voices and sounds of outsiders: the black slang, the Latin beat, the worries of teenagers. As the original version of 'Hound Dog' showed, the anguish of a woman, exploited by a selfish male, was given voice by Leiber and Stoller. Their naughty-boy humour did not descend to misogyny. If they ogle women, they do not downgrade them. 'Little Egypt', another hit for the Coasters, describes a scantily clad, belly dancer doing her routine. The singer describes how transfixed he was. The catch comes in the ending. He falls in love with the dancer; they marry and have seven children, who now are learning to dance like their mother.

No-one is excluded in this music. There are even sly references to homosexuality — so sly that they were able to slink past the moral orthodoxies of the time. Leiber and Stoller were asked to write the songs for Elvis's film *Jailhouse Rock*. The title song depicts a rocking party in the jail. It has to be an all-male party, given that its participants are prisoners and warders. The song is an invitation to join in the fun of this party.

In one of the verses, a prisoner is described as telling another that he is the "cutest jailbird" he's ever seen and that he would be delighted to share his company. Elvis sang the verse straight. Jerry Lee Lewis, in his version,

58

puts on a knowing, high-pitched, effeminate voice for these words. But he can't distance himself from the invitation. All are invited to join in the Jailhouse Rock: the singer, the audience, the warders, the prisoners, even the cutest jailbird. The writers are inviting, not censoring, the outcasts.

Nelson George has written of Leiber and Stoller's "uncanny ability" to write from the perspective of blacks.[29] The talent might be uncanny, as talent usually is. But the basis of the talent is not. It was not cool to write from the perspective of Jewish teenagers — so another idiom had to be found. If Leiber used the particular slang of young blacks, then this was employed to describe feelings that all young people shared. In some matters, the Jewish and black worlds overlapped in those days. Young Jews, such as Leiber and Stoller, would know where racism and bigotry led. Their parents and grandparents would remind them continually, thereby communicating a distrust of the established world — the WASP world. Poor white Southerners such as Elvis would not have this knowledge continually reaffirmed in their childhood. No signed picture of Gershwin, who consciously combined black jazz and European classical music, hung in the Presley family shack.

Leiber and Stoller could use their own experiences, even as they were writing for others. 'On Broadway' depicts a man who has come to the city in search of success, but who is destitute on the streets. The singer claims just to have one thin dime — not even enough to shine his shoes. The people back home say he won't last in the city. He'll have to get a Greyhound bus and head for home.

The song is written from the perspective of those who have to travel by bus. They are poor, but not absolutely destitute. They can't afford cars or planes, but they have enough for a Greyhound bus ticket. It was by Greyhound

---

29. George, *The Death of Rhythm and Blues*, p61.

bus that the Leibers travelled from Baltimore to California. It's the detail — it's not just a bus, but specifically a Greyhound bus — that always lifts Leiber and Stoller songs above cliché and sets them in the lived world.

Nearly thirty years after Elvis's success with 'Hound Dog', the songs of Leiber and Stoller were put together for a Broadway musical *Smokey Joe's Cafe* (which is the title of one of their early compositions for the Robins). It is ironic that Elvis's 'Hound Dog', when first released, seemed to be sweeping aside the old traditions exemplified by the Broadway musical. Sometimes, when revolution is loudly and urgently declared, it takes a generation to notice the patterns of continuity beneath the obvious signs of rupture. Leiber and Stoller, in some respects, not least by their own backgrounds, do not stand apart from that earlier tradition. What were *King Creole* and *Jailhouse Rock*, if not musicals? Like Harold Arlen before them, Leiber and Stoller steeped themselves in African American music, taking pride in writing for the best black singers. And like Arlen, they did not just copy; they innovated.

In their work as writers and producers, Leiber and Stoller worked against narrow prejudices which separated music into an apartheid of racial categories. It was entirely fitting that *Smokey Joe's Cafe* should quite unremarkably be performed by a mixed cast of young black and white performers, dancing and singing on stage together. The show might have been tapping nostalgia, but what was natural in the late 1990s would have been unthinkable when Leiber and Stoller first started writing for Willie Mae Thornton.

Jewish Soul Men

4

Leiber and Stoller were not the only city Jews who were being drawn to rhythm and blues in the 1950s. Others had trodden a similar path, working with obscure black artists in the years before Elvis achieved international fame. In fact, there was a bunch of composers and producers who shared a passion for African American music. They tended to know and work with each other. Some have already been mentioned in passing, such as Doc Pomus, who wrote prolifically for Elvis. Also there was Jerry Wexler, the man who negotiated a deal for Leiber and Stoller at Atlantic Records and who so disliked their first recording with the Drifters. Wexler's work was to be influential in developing rhythm and blues into what has become generally known as 'soul music'.

Much of the work of the Jewish 'soul men' was conducted behind the scenes. These were not men (and this is principally a story of males, not females) who performed publicly. Some of their work was for black singers. Some was for the white hit-makers, whose image fitted the WASPish culture of those times. Some of the less well-known work would be rediscovered in the 1960s, especially by English groups. Young white musicians were listening to recordings on small black labels. There they found seemingly neglected gems, which they incorporated into their own repertoires and then recorded to great acclaim.

In this way, the Beatles rediscovered Leiber and Stoller's 'Kansas City'. Their big 'black' find was 'Twist And Shout', which they knew from the old Isley Brothers' recording. No early Beatles concert would be complete without the rising crescendo of the song. One critic has commented that Lennon's delivery was "nothing short of lustful".[1] It was infinitely more dangerous music than the tunes that Lennon and McCartney themselves were writing in the early years. The Rolling Stones, to an even greater extent than the Beatles, brought the music of black rhythm and blues to a white audience. Their first American hit was 'Time Is On My Side', originally recorded by Irma Thomas for the American black market. Then, there was Janis Joplin, whose most famous song, 'Piece Of My Heart', had been composed for Erma Franklin.

The list could go on. Those sixties white mega-stars were bringing 'black' music to a huge white audience. But, again, it was not always quite as it seemed. Afficianados of the Beatles or the Stones might know that their heroes were singing an Isley Brothers or an Irma Thomas song. But they would be less likely to know the identity of the composers. It may come as a surprise that the 'black' songs just mentioned—'Twist And Shout', 'Piece Of My Heart', 'Time Is On My Side'—were not 'pure' African American music. Their origins are to be traced not so much to the black exodus from the Deep South, but to an earlier exodus from central Europe.

It was Willie Mae and Elvis all over again — with the composers being ignored. On the sliding scale of rock celebrity, the WASPish performer was well out in front. Then came the black performer. The Jewish composer barely registers on the celebrity scale, but is, nevertheless, still ahead of the underpaid (or rather unpaid) black composer. It was very different from the thirties, when the fame of the Jewish composer could out-dazzle the singers.

---

1. Rile, T. (1988) *Tell Me Why: a Beatles commentary*. London: Bodley Head, p60.

Doc Pomus

Leiber and Stoller were following a path that had already been taken by Doc Pomus. He, too, came to the world of black rhythm and blues as a young man. Later, like Leiber and Stoller, he was to write hits for Elvis. Some of his well-known Elvis songs were mentioned at the start of the previous chapter. Pomus's songs for Elvis, however, were only a small part of a massive output that helped to create the sound of early rock. His music is utterly familiar to a whole generation, but his name remains little known.

Doc Pomus was born as Jerome Solon Felder in 1925 in Brooklyn, New York. His parents had hoped that their son might go to college to become a doctor or accountant. It was a common hope for that generation of Jewish parents, who wanted their children to gain the sort of professional security that they had been denied. It was always going to be a struggle for the young Jerome. As a child, he was struck by polio, leaving him crippled. At school, he acquired the nickname 'Doc', not because he seemed destined for the medical career, which would have delighted his parents, but because of his readiness to offer wise advice to his contemporaries.

In his teens, Doc was drawn to the demi-monde of rhythm clubs and gambling joints. The love of the night world was never to leave him. His life, he often recounted, was transformed by hearing the rhythm and blues of Big Joe Turner, the great 'blues shouter', whose style was such a forerunner to rock. How could the solid world of accountancy compete with the excitement and the pain of the blues? Soon Doc was writing and singing rhythm and blues. The early photographs show a short, black-haired, swarthy young man, singing into a free-standing microphone, supporting himself on wooden crutches.[2]

---

2. For a lovely tribute to Doc Pomus, see the liner notes written by Gerri Hirshey on the Pomus tribute album *Till The Night Is Gone* (Rhino Records, 1995).

At this time, he changed his name from Felder to Pomus. He said that he did not want his parents to know that he was spending his evenings singing in less than respectable clubs. It's a good story. Perhaps it is the literal truth. However, decisions can be multiply determined. Doc's change of name fits a wider pattern of Jewish performers discarding obviously Jewish names. There would be little mileage for a blues singer called Felder, especially if he were, in Pomus's own words, a 'cripple'. If he had merely wished to escape his parents' notice, he could have swapped one Jewish surname for another. But he became Pomus, rather than Levy or Weinstein. This was a more general trend. Bernard Schwartz, who was born in the same year as Doc, became Tony Curtis. No aspiring performer, whether actor or singer, born with the surname of Curtis, would have dreamt of adopting the stage name of Schwartz.

Jewish performers might have felt the need to discard their Jewish surnames, but songwriters, not taking the public eye, felt less pressure to discard the give-away labels of ethnicity. Leiber and Stoller had no reason to find more anglo stage names. They could even play jokes with Jewish pseudonyms. For the credits of 'Dance With Me', they humorously styled themselves as Louis Lebish and Irv Nathan. Doc Pomus retained his stage name even after he had given up his performing in the late forties in order to concentrate on songwriting.

Initially, in the pre-Presley era, he was writing specifically for rhythm and blues artists. In particular, Pomus provided his idol, Joe Turner, with 'Boogie Woogie Country Girl'. Turner recorded other Pomus compositions, such as 'Don't You Cry' and 'Still In Love'. Pomus was delighted when Ray Charles turned 'Lonely Avenue' into an R&B hit in 1956. Pomus was to remain a life-long admirer and friend of Charles.

After the advent of rock, Pomus felt that he needed a younger collaborator to help him keep abreast of changing tastes. He teamed up with the Mort Shuman, who was from Brooklyn and who was eleven years Doc's junior. The choice was felicitous. Mort Shuman had studied classical music at the New York Conservatory and was an accomplished pianist. Together, Pomus and Shuman wrote over twenty songs for Elvis, including hard rockers, such as 'A Mess Of Blues', and softer numbers such as 'Surrender'.

Pomus also contributed to Leiber and Stoller's work with the Coasters. He gave them the half-written 'Young Blood', in which a shy boy sings about his nervousness in approaching a girl. Leiber and Stoller turned to Pomus and Shuman to write songs for the Drifters, whose records they were producing. The result was a series of catchy love songs such as 'This Magic Moment', 'I Count The Tears' and 'Sweets For My Sweet' — all of which were top twenty hits in the US. Regarding 'Sweets For My Sweet', which was very different from the intense blues songs that Pomus had written for Ray Charles, Doc said "sometimes the superego has to take a holiday".

Pomus's words, like those of Leiber, were not mere frothy pop. His songs managed to combine catchy, seemingly light melodies with a sense of depth. He understood that the happy moment could be filled with sadness. 'Save The Last Dance For Me' was Pomus and Shuman's biggest hit for the Drifters, going to number one in the US. Jerry Leiber has said that he knew it was a hit the moment he first heard the opening bars.[3] The song can be enjoyed as a happy Latin-rock tune about dancing and sparkling wine. The chorus is unforgettable. But there is an undertow. A man is recognizing that his lover must dance with other men: Go on, he tells her, enjoy the excitement of the moment. As he watches her dance, he hopes that she will remember to save the last dance for him. The polio-stricken Pomus, of course, knew what it was like to have

---

3. Wexler, J. and Ritz, D. (1994) *Rhythm and the Blues: a life in American music*. London: Jonathan Cape, p137.

to sit and watch while others, including his own wife, danced. The song was, according to Leiber "a poignant piece of personal poetry".

Hits were written for a variety of young stars. Dion, for instance, had success with Pomus and Shuman songs, such as 'Teenager In Love'. Astute management selected Fabian for instant stardom because he looked the part with his well-groomed hair and pretty-boy face. The star, who could hardly sing, needed material. So, the management turned to Pomus. The short, overweight, thirty-something Jewish 'cripple', who most certainly could not be presented as a rock star, duly obliged. Fabian had his hits — 'Turn Me Loose', 'I'm A Man', 'Hound Dog Man'. The episode reveals much about the hidden and publicly presentable faces of rock at that time.

The list of singers who have recorded Pomus songs, reads like a history of contemporary popular music. Apart from Elvis Presley, there are the Beatles, Marvin Gaye, Bob Marley, Dolly Parton, Bruce Springsteen, Jerry Lee Lewis, ZZ Top, Elvis Costello, Andy Williams and so on. Over one hundred and fifty million recordings of Pomus songs have been sold, with over a hundred Top 100 US single hits.

After 1965, Pomus's output tailed off. He and Shuman split. Shuman went to England to collaborate with other writers and then to France to work with the French composer Jacques Brel. Pomus suffered a severe fall, which resulted in his exchanging crutches for confinement to a wheelchair. He spent much of the next ten years as a professional gambler. Unlike Leiber and Stoller, and other producers and writers, he did not go into management or company-ownership.

Eventually, Doc Pomus returned to the blues, which was his first and greatest musical love. He continued to derive intense pride when his songs were recorded by great blues singers. B.B. King recorded an album of his songs, including 'There Must Be A Better World Somewhere'. It is said that King, having recorded the song, broke down and cried for over an hour. He was moved by the depth of a song whose deceptively simple words, while telling of present sadness, look forward to a world freed from the failures of the present.

Pomus remained a fiercely independent character with a wide circle of friends. Generous of spirit and with a keen sense of justice, he established charities to help those blues singers who, despite the greatness of their works, were living in poverty. Nothing made him angrier than to see bootleg versions of old blues songs. These great artists were not just cheated in life, he would complain, but cheated in death. As Jerry Wexler of Atlantic Records said, "if the music industry had a heart, it would have been Doc Pomus".[4]

Pomus often said that he wished "to be larger than life, a man amongst men". The tributes that poured in after his death from cancer in March 1991 testified to what extent that ambition had been realized.[5] He had become a hero to a younger generation of songwriters. Lou Reed, for one, called him "a great songwriter, poet, philanthropist, gambler and raconteur supreme... a blazing sun, an exploding star". For Phil Spector, Pomus was, quite simply, "the greatest songwriter that ever lived". Even in his last days in hospital, he was writing blues with the New Orleans pianist, Dr John. 1991 was not a good year. In November, Mort Shuman died from a liver disease at the age of fifty-four.

It was not surprising that Pomus became the first white man to be honoured by the Rhythm and Blues Foundation's Pioneer Award. *Rolling Stone* was not exaggerating when it declared in its obituary that "every songwriter in Rock & Roll owes something to Doc Pomus" for Doc "helped invent Rock & Roll". The question is whether Pomus's background, and that of those other pioneers,

---

4. Wexler and Ritz, p137.
5. For a compilation of tributes and other quotes about Pomus, see 'The Official Doc Pomus Web Site': http://www.felderpomus.com.

Leiber and Stoller, is a mere coincidence. Did it have to be a Jew who would be the first white so honoured by the Rhythm and Blues Foundation? Could non-Jews have created the syntheses pioneered by these writers? What would rock'n'roll have been like without these Jewish inventors? The questions are unanswerable. We cannot know what the history of rock would have been like without its Jewish composers. All we can say is that those composers are at the centre of rock's early story. Without them, the story would be different.

Pomus's work shares the same sort of moral vision that is contained in Leiber and Stoller's. Theirs is a music for all, on the side of the weak against the strong. True, Pomus rarely wrote songs specifically for women singers — that was the climate of the times. Yet the songs, with their universal message, do not belong to one type of voice. Just listen to Tina Turner singing 'Save The Last Dance For Me' or Irma Thomas's version of 'There Must Be A Better World'. The words now tell a women's story, with depth and sympathy.

The songs carry no overtly propagandist message, yet they express a sense of justice that contains no meanness or exclusivity. They represent a humanity and pleasure that must always oppose the forces of bigotry. This is not an unthinking pleasure, although from time to time the superego must go on holiday. There is an understanding of the limits of pleasure: as one person dances with joy, another is condemned merely to watch and hope. The moments of joy come with an understanding, ingrained in the heritage of the blues and in the traditions of all historically oppressed groups, that there should be a better world.

Jerry Wexler

Just as the English language owes a debt to Alan Freed for inventing the term 'rock'n'roll', so the origins of the phrase

'rhythm and blues' can be accredited to another Jew: Jerry
Wexler. However, Wexler's contribution to R&B is not
solely linguistic. He was one of the key figures in creating
the sounds of soul music and, through his involvement with
Atlantic records, he helped shape the rock industry.

Wexler, like Pomus, came to rock via an enthusiasm for
black American music. He was born in 1917 in New York
City, the older son of Jewish immigrants.[6] His father,
Harry Wexler, was an immigrant from Poland, while his
mother's family, a cut above his father's, was from Germany. Harry, like many Jewish immigrants of that time,
struggled to make a living. He washed windows. His wife,
Elsa, made sure their sons knew that she expected something better from them.

Harry Wexler had been brought up in an orthodox family in a traditional *shtetl*. One of the first things that he
had done on arriving in the States, was to shave off his
payess, or long sidelocks. It was a symbolic gesture as
much as anything: like so many young immigrants of that
period, he was determined to plunge into the life of the
New World. Despite discarding the outward signs of religion, not all was, or could be, sloughed off. It would have
been virtually unthinkable for a Jew like Harry Wexler to
have married out.

So, Harry married Elsa and lived among Jews. Their
sons were to be brought up with a strong Jewish consciousness. Jerry had a Bar Mitzvah, although there was a
family argument whether it should be in an orthodox synagogue, as his father's side of the family wanted, or in a
reform synagogue. Culturally, Jerry's upbringing and
neighbourhood circle was overwhelmingly Jewish. He
would have grown up hearing Yiddish words and melodies
from the Old World, while all the time being drawn out-
wards to the dangerous world of gentiles.

---

6. The background details are contained in Wexler's autobiography:
Wexler and Ritz, *Rhythm and the Blues*.

Jerry's mother had ambitions for her sons. She wanted them to be doctors, dentists or great literary figures. Despite her best efforts, Jerry was not a model student. He would not stay home studying his books. He was forever hanging out with the wrong sort of boys, visiting Harlem and listening to jazz. His mother persuaded him to give college a try. She took him to visit Kansas State College for an interview with the chairman of the journalism department. In his autobiography, Jerry recounts how the chairman, an old-style Protestant American, turned out to have a Jewish wife. This reassured his mother, but at the same time worried her. She asked the academic if his career would be damaged because of prejudice by the academic establishment against his Jewish wife. "A half a century later", Wexler wrote, I can still see him rising from the table, reaching for his goblet of wine, and announcing, 'Here's the bottle, and here's the glass — if they don't like it they can kiss my ass'".[7]

The story reveals much about those times. We see a Jewish mother, whose ambitions are pushing her son into an alien world which would discriminate against Jews. She does not hide her fears from her son. In his hearing, she fears that being Jewish — or even having a Jewish wife — will be a barrier in the very world she wants her son to join. Jerry knows that he is being pushed into unsafe territory. To remain stuck in the window-washing world of Harry Wexler would be dangerous — and moving forward would be to step into the unknown. There was no easy escape.

There is evidence that some American Jews of Wexler's generation entered the world of music as a consequence of anti-semitism in institutions of higher education. Larry Adler, the harmonica player, is a case in point. Initially he wanted to become a civil engineer. He was to claim that he would never have taken up music professionally had the

---

7. Wexler and Ritz, p29.

local college in Baltimore admitted Jews to its engineering courses.[8]

In Jerry Wexler's case, life at college did not go well. He could not settle. His grades deteriorated and at the end of his second year, his mother fetched him back. His father appears to have taken no part in these educational decisions. The war followed and Jerry served in the army. Afterwards, he completed his degree course. Meanwhile, jazz seems to have increasingly occupied his attention. His ambition now was to obtain work in the music business.

The Jewish networks in the music industry were to come to Jerry's aid, enabling him to put adolescent dreams into practice. As it was, someone knew someone who knew someone who could find him a job. So Jerry managed to secure a position as a journalist on the music magazine *Billboard*. There, he came under the influence of Paul Ackerman, another Jew, who found no problem in loving music of all types. According to Wexler, Ackerman's deep knowledge of jazz, blues and country music was allied to the classical culture of his German-Jewish background. As Wexler was to write, "few people have affected me as profoundly as Paul"; so Ackerman became Wexler's "guru" in music and in life.[9]

It was while writing for *Billboard* that Wexler stopped using the conventional term 'Race' music, which he found offensive and demeaning. In its place, he invented 'rhythm & blues' in order to describe the music that he was being drawn towards. More contacts led to further job offers. In 1952, Ahmet Ertegun and Herb Abramson, the owners of the independent label Atlantic Records, offered Jerry a position. Abramson was Jewish, while Ertegun, a different sort of outsider, was the son of a former Turkish ambassador. Miriam Abramson, Herb's wife, was also to

8. Freedland, *So Let's Hear the Applause*, p204.
9. Wexler and Ritz, pp. 59f.

play an important part in the company.[10] Atlantic were recording black blues, boogie and jazz, aimed at a black audience. As Wexler noted, there was then no thought of selling black music to whites.[11] Originally hired for the promotion side of the business, Wexler was taken on as a partner. Soon he was working in the studios, producing records.

Many years later, Wexler distinguished between different types of producers. Some producers, he said, were essentially 'documentarian'. Leonard Chess, for example, would hear Muddy Waters play in a bar one night, and then the next day he would attempt to capture the same sound in the studio. The recording thus aimed to document the live performance of the artist. Wexler, on the other hand, developed a more creative style, so that the process of recording would develop the repertoire and range of the performer. The producer would suggest tunes for the singer, plan the arrangements and generally supervise the recording so that the whole process would enhance what the artist could do. The trick was to serve the artist's talent, bringing out inner possibilities, rather than imposing pre-set ideas or merely reproducing what the singer was already doing. All the time, the aim was to produce music of the highest possible quality.[12]

Wexler has said that his encyclopaedic knowledge of jazz was essential. He would be able to make suggestions to blues men, proposing, for instance, jazz riffs, which he had heard on obscure recordings and which the blues musicians might not know. This recycling of music was not theft. This sort of borrowing has been part and parcel of popular music from years before the idea of copyright had ever been imagined. Wexler's borrowings were both a

---

10. For a history of Atlantic Records, see Gillett, C. (1986) *Making Tracks: the story of Atlantic Records*. London: Souvenir Press.
11. Wexler and Ritz, p79.
12. Buskin, R. (1999) 'Jerry Wexler: Atlantic adventure', *Studio Sound*, April.

tribute and a creative act. By synthesising elements of the African American past and by colouring it with the present musician's contribution, the music could move forward. This was very different from those white imitations of black rock, which reproduced arrangements and delivery note for note, while subtracting all the dangerous passion.

Again and again, Wexler was to apply his philosophy of recording to the work of black artists, putting his knowledge at their disposal. Some artists, such as Ray Charles, did not need such direction and he, in fact, resisted it, having a clear idea of the music he wanted to produce. Others worked with Wexler, so that the collaboration resulted in recordings that transcended the live performances the artists had been capable of producing. The result was that Atlantic built up a unique collection of soul, rhythm & blues, pop and rock recordings, that quite literally transformed the sound of popular music.

To begin with, Wexler worked mainly with pre-rock rhythm and blues artists, such as T-Bone Walker, Big Joe Turner and Champion Jack Dupree. Atlantic branched out into more pop-orientated rock, again specialising in recording black singers. It was the classic recording of the Drifters that kept the company financially buoyant in the late fifties — whatever Wexler thought about 'There Goes My Baby', the first of the re-formed Drifters' successes. For these recordings, Leiber and Stoller worked as writers and producers. Burt Bacharach was also commissioned to work on the Drifters' records. Doc Pomus was hired to write hits for the group and so were younger songwriters, who were predominantly Jewish and whose work will be discussed in the following chapter.

Wexler tended to distance himself from the Drifters' records. They were too poppy, too filled with violins, for his taste. He was developing a tight brassy sound with a strong bass line. The bass was all important. He claimed that the emphasis on bass differentiated R&B from both jazz and pop: "When most of us go to record an R&B tune

we look for a strong bass line".[13] This is the sound for
which he made Atlantic famous. Wexler, very much in the
tradition of Gershwin, mixed the music up. He was not
bound by conventional categories. Solomon Burke was one
of the major soul singers signed to Atlantic. He styled himself as the 'King of Soul'n'Rock' appearing on stage with
regal crown and cape. His first big hit on Atlantic, suggested by Wexler, was, in fact, a country and western song
'Just Out Of Reach'. Burke, of course, did not sing it in
conventional country style. Wexler was not the only Jewish producer mixing up country and R&B. Syd Nathan of
King Records, who produced the early James Brown
records, encouraged R&B singers to record hillbilly music
and vice versa.[14]

Wexler also became involved with Stax Records, a small
independent label operating out of Memphis. Stax was
making important soul recordings, including those of Otis
Redding and Booker T and the MGs. Owned by Estelle
Axton and her brother Jim Stewart, Stax was encouraging
black and white artists to work together in a racially
divided city. Wexler recognized the potential and the originality of the recordings. Stax became a subsidiary of
Atlantic and Wexler travelled south to help out in the
recording sessions, particularly those of the new discovery
Wilson Pickett.

Although Stax's music-making crossed racial barriers,
the wider atmosphere of Memphis and the south could not
be prevented from seeping into the studios. There were
tensions in the Stax 'family'. It is said that Jim Stewart,
who directed musical operations, tended not to invite
black musicians to his home; and there were, at that time,

---

13. Quoted in Millar, *The Drifters*. London: Studio Vista p84.
14. Guralnick, P. (1986) *Sweet Soul Music: Rhythm and Blues and the
    Southern dream of freedom*. London: Virgin Books, p226. Perhaps the
    most famous mixing of country and R&B was Ray Charles's album
    Modern Sounds In Country And Western, recorded in 1962 after
    Charles had left Atlantic.

few public places where blacks and whites could meet socially with ease.[15]

According to one Memphis musician, Stewart's Stax recordings were taking place in a "racially aggressive situation".[16] Wexler breezed in. Nobody was going to tell him where he could, and could not, meet musicians. Peter Guralnick, in his book *Sweet Soul Music*, has described Wexler at Stax. Singers like Wilson Pickett were not treated as stars by the Stax personnel — after all, Pickett, like the rest of them, was just a local guy. Wexler was the star: "Jerry Wexler was an exotic presence; his very speech (a 'Jewish brogue') was like a foreign tongue to Memphians, who had never even seen New York City".[17]

One can imagine the scene. There was Wexler, the foreigner, the outsider — white but not exactly so, at least in a Southern way — acting as catalyst. He could barge through the Southern etiquettes of race. He would be the dominating presence, making suggestions, criticising and encouraging everyone, regardless of race. He would know more about black music than most of the black musicians and take command more naturally than any white Southerner such as Jim Stewart, who had had been brought up to take racial command. His obvious Jewishness — his Jewish brogue — was all part of this.

More than anything, Wexler's name and that of Atlantic are associated with Aretha Franklin, indisputably 'The Queen of Soul'. As Nelson Goodman has written, "if anyone wondered what 'soul' was, all they had to do was play any of Aretha Franklin's Atlantic albums".[18] Mostly, Wexler recorded her in studios in Muscle Shoals, Alabama, using session musicians, both white and black, to bring out Franklin's extraordinary vocal range and intensity of feeling. She recorded a vari-

15. Guralnick, *Sweet Soul Music*, p106.
16. Guralnick, *Sweet Soul Music*, p153.
17. Guralnick, *Sweet Soul Music*, p155.
18. George, *The Death of Rhythm & Blues*, p105.

ety of songs, including classic black gospel and rhythm and blues.

In addition, other songs came to Aretha Franklin via Wexler's network of Jewish composers. She did a cover version of Burt Bacharach and Hal David's 'I Say A Little Prayer'. Originally the song had been recorded by Dionne Warwick, a softer black singer who had come to Atlantic's notice as a backing singer on some of the Drifters' recordings. Warwick regularly recorded Bacharach and David's songs (such as 'Walk On By', 'Do You Know The Way To San José?', 'Trains And Boats and Planes')—another creative example of black performance and Jewish writing. Bacharach and David, of course, also had a stream of hits with white artists, such as '24 Hours From Tulsa' (Gene Pitney), 'Make It Easy On Yourself' (Walker Brothers), 'What's New Pussycat?' (Tom Jones). Wexler also commissioned Carole King and Gerry Goffin to write for Aretha Franklin. Wexler gave them the title '(You Make Me Feel Like) A Natural Woman' and asked them to fashion it into a song for Aretha. Wexler, who dreamt up the title line, is credited as the third author. The song was to become an Aretha Franklin classic. In Wexler's words, "the song has become part of Aretha's own persona, a product of her own soul".[19]

How, one might ask, could a song written by white Jewish composers become a product of the Queen of Soul's own soul? Unless the claim is completely spurious, some simultaneous currents — both personal and historical — must have been at work. A hint can be given, to show how Franklin and Wexler's lives were being carried forward by momentarily parallel, but different, forces of history.

Aretha Franklin's father, a pastor at Detroit's New Bethel Baptist Church, was a close friend of Martin Luther King. The Reverend Franklin was well-known in

19. Wexler and Ritz, p214.

black religious circles for his radio preaching. Aretha, too, was committed to King's movement. In February 1968, just months before his death, Martin Luther King presented Aretha Franklin with a special award for her work in the civil rights movement. She was to sing at King's funeral.

The civil rights movement, under Martin Luther King's leadership, was primarily assimilationist in that it sought to break down the barriers which were preventing the integration of blacks into mainstream American society. Young Jews from the north were quick to join the early civil rights marches in the south. During the early sixties, they were especially involved in the movement to register blacks as voters in the Deep South.

Assimilation as a goal, and as a condition of life, was something that Wexler well understood. As a secular Jew, he had spent his life assimilating, even in the face of prejudice. He had gone to Kansas State College; but he had not advanced as his mother would have wished in the Protestant world of old America. Yet he had become American, immersing himself in American music, just as Gershwin and Arlen had done. His autobiography carries the significant subtitle 'A life in American music'. His American music was not that of the old order which would have looked down upon his window-washing father. Nor, of course, was it the music of the cantors, that his father had decisively rejected. It was the music of the one group, above all, that continued to suffer the sort of discrimination in the New World that his own parents, and those of his childhood friends, had escaped in the Old World.

In 1930, Isaac Goldberg, a Jewish author writing on Tin Pan Alley in a book commended by George Gershwin, commented on the importance of Jewish composers as well as 'Negroes' for the development of popular music. Goldberg asked: What did the two 'races' share? He offered an answer to his own question: both partook of "the sad, the

77

hysterical psychology of the oppressed race".[20] Goldberg's psychology may be somewhat naive. Oppression does not necessarily breed hysteria. Nor are the effects of oppression uniform. However, at particular junctures of history, and in specific places, parallel histories of oppression can coalesce into an alliance, if not of shared experience, at least of personal and aesthetic understanding.

As was mentioned earlier, Doc Pomus was the first white to be honoured by the Rhythm and Blues Foundation. The possibility of a random throw of the ethnic dice was reduced further, when Jerry Wexler, another Jew, became in 1995 the first white recipient of the Blues Foundation Lifetime Achievement Award. Perhaps, it is not surprising that Wexler should look for, and find, poetry in the music of the oppressed. Everything in his life had taught him to distrust the lofty judgments of the powers that be. Neither Aretha Franklin's music, nor her politics, could have been a threat to him, as they were to those whites who accepted unquestioningly the politics of racial hierarchy.

Wexler recalls that Franklin did not discuss her politics with him. There was some political reserve in their relationship, at least on her part. Yet, coming from a politically aware background, she may have felt that crude, racist politics would not find a home in the studio of a Jew who loved the music of African Americans as his own American music.[21] If this is the case, then the partnership did not merely reflect the particularities of two strong and

20. Goldberg, I. (1930/1961) *Tin Pan Alley: a chronicle of American popular music*. New York: Fred Ungar, p293. George Gershwin wrote the preface for the book.
21. There is evidence that Wexler did not tolerate racist behaviour. Once he was producing Aretha Franklin at Ricky Hall's Muscle Shoals studios and Hall began arguing with Franklin's husband. The argument continued into the evening and degenerated into racist name calling. Franklin and her husband abruptly left the next morning, breaking off the recording session. Wexler was incensed with Hall and finished recording Franklin in New York (for details see Wexler and Ritz, *Rhythm and the Blues*, pp. 210f and Guralnick, *Sweet Soul Music*, pp. 342f).

talented personalities. It was backed by the forces of a wider history as the two created a brief alliance of creativity.

Berns and Ragovoy

Aretha Franklin came from a family steeped in music. Her father made numerous religious records. Her mother, who left home when Aretha was six, was said to have had a voice similar to the future 'Queen of Soul'.[22] All three daughters were singers, although Carolyn and Erma did not achieve the success of Aretha. However, Erma recorded the classic soul song 'Piece Of My Heart', which is as good as any soul record and which is deservedly to be found on most 'greatest hits' soul compilations.

Erma Franklin's 'Piece Of My Heart' may be a great tune, sung to perfection, but it took a white singer to bring the song to a wider audience. It was like Elvis and 'Hound Dog' replayed a decade later — and again with a hidden Jewish dimension. If Elvis was, in the words of Sam Phillips, a white who sang like a black man, then Janis Joplin projected herself as having the voice and inner tragedy of a black blues singer. In the late sixties, her emotional delivery became a feature of a number of major sixties pop festivals, which were, of course, predominantly white events. 'Piece Of My Heart' became the high spot of her appearances.

Joplin had a short life, dying of a drugs overdose in 1970 at the age of twenty-seven. Since then, she has attained almost mythic status, as the fragile singer who lived, and died, for her art. As is typical, Hollywood cannot leave a myth alone. Plans to make a film of Joplin's life were reported in 1997. It was said that Melissa Etheridge was in negotiations with Lakeshore Entertainments to star in the

---

22. Guralnick, *Sweet Soul Music*, p333.

'biop'. The rumour was that the company was willing to pay over one million dollars for the rights to use 'Piece Of My Heart'. If true, this would represent one of the most expensive licensing fees for a song in Hollywood's history.[23]

Among critics, there has been debate about the quality of Joplin's singing. Was she a genuine soul singer? Or was she debasing black music? It's essentially the same debate about Presley's qualities. Brian Ward in *Just My Soul Responding* puts the case for the prosecution. He analyses Joplin's style mercilessly. Her frenzied screechings and projections of rampant sexuality were little more than "enactments of white stereotypes", as she publicly performed the raw, uncontrolled emotion that whites expected to govern the lives of blacks, especially black women. According to Ward, Joplin showed "little appreciation of the understatement, the subtle phrasing and manipulation of dramatic tensions" that were central to black blues — and which were of course, displayed at their finest in the music of Aretha Franklin. Unwittingly, Joplin's performance, according to Ward, resembled the nineteenth century minstrels, as she "desperately sought to capture the essence of the black experience as defined by whites".[24]

If Joplin aimed to capture such an 'essence' of black experience, then what is often unnoticed is how many of her songs had Jewish origins. 'Piece Of My Heart' did not have an 'authentic' black composer. It was written by Bert Berns and Jerry Ragovoy. On a recent budget price CD, 'The Very Best of Janis Joplin', four of the twelve songs were written or co-written by Jerry Ragovoy; a fifth is

---

23. An earlier film, 'The Rose', was a fictional story loosely based on Joplin's life. The film, released in 1979, starred Bette Midler, who is Jewish. However, neither the film, nor Midler's subsequent album of the same name, contained Joplin's music. There was no 'Piece Of My Heart', nor other Joplin favourites.
24. Ward, B. (1998). *Just My Soul Responding: rhthym and blues, Black consciousness and race relations.* Berkeley: University of California, p248.

Gershwin's classic 'Summertime', another song written by a Jew for a black voice.[25] Ragovoy combined with Mort Shuman to write 'Get It While You Can' — a song which was originally recorded by Howard Tate. Garnett Mimms was the original singer of 'Cry Baby', another Joplin favourite, which was written by Berns and Ragovoy.

The name of Wexler is well known among followers of soul music. By contrast, Bert Russell Berns and Jerry Ragovoy are hardly household names. But both deserve attention, and not merely for their contribution to Joplin's oeuvre.

Berns was the man whom Wexler describes as his "first protégé".[26] He was a songwriter, producer and generally awkward customer. Several of his songs have become classics, most notably 'Twist And Shout', whose history also resembles that of 'Hound Dog'. The original 'black' recordings — first by the Top Notes and then by the Isley Brothers — had limited success. It was only when the Beatles took up the song that 'Twist and Shout' emerged from obscurity. Today, millions may know the song intimately. It is unlikely that many could name Berns as composer, nor that they would be able to identify his background.

Like Wexler, Berns was a second generation immigrant. He was born in the Bronx in 1929 to immigrant Russian parents, who ran a small dress shop. Wexler describes him as a "homeboy": Wexler's father used to clean the windows of the Berns' shop.[27] In common with Mike Stoller and Mort Shuman, Berns learnt classical piano. In fact, he studied at the Juillard School of Music.[28] During his teenage years, however, Bert was drawn to a different type of music.[29] He would haunt the Puerto

---

25. Actually, only two of the songs have black composers. Joplin herself wrote, or co-wrote, four of the songs and a fifth comes from the country singer Kris Kristofferson.
26. Wexler and Ritz, p153.
27. Wexler and Ritz, p153
28. Millar, B. (1971) *The Drifters*, p85.
29. See web homepage on Bert Berns, prepared by Brett Berns.

Rican salsa clubs of New York. He was also hanging out with some dubious characters.

His role model would be George Goldner, a New York Jew of Wexler's generation. Goldner had a fascination with Latin-American music. His wife was Latina and he founded his own record label — Tico — to record mamba music. Through the black craze for mamba in the early fifties, Goldner had become introduced to black urban blues. He set up a succession of small labels for recording black artists. His greatest success was the discovery of Frankie Lymon and the Teenagers. Goldner is credited with being the writer of their biggest hit 'Why Do Fools Fall In Love'. It is now too long since then to say whether he deserved that credit. Certainly, during his lifetime, Goldner had a reputation for genuinely loving Latino music, as well as enjoying the wheeling and dealing of the music business's outer edges.

Berns, too, had a fascination with the world of hustlers and shady night-clubs, combined with a love of Latin-American music. It appears that Berns spent some time in pre-Castro Cuba, although quite what he was doing is unclear. He liked to spread stories of underworld dealings. Wexler comments on Berns's capacity for "romantic exaggeration", but adds that "his feeling for Latin rhythms was right as rain".[30]

Berns worked for the music publishers Mellin for seven years, writing under several names including Bert Russell and Russell Byrd. Primarily, he wrote for black soul singers, such as Garnet Mimms, as well as for the Isley Brothers, whose recordings he produced. Wexler took him on at Atlantic, both as a writer and producer, recognizing his talent to combine black and Latino influences. 'Twist And Shout' illustrates this synthesis. The verse and chorus come out of the secularised gospel tradition, while the instrumental break

---

30. Wexler and Ritz, p155.

goes into a 'La Bamba' rhythm. And it all fits together perfectly.

When Leiber and Stoller gave up producing the Drifters' records, Berns was able to fill the gap more than adequately. It was Berns, for example, who produced 'Under The Boardwalk'. Berns also produced the soul singer Solomon Burke, co-writing several of his successful songs. As Wexler recounts, Berns's relationship with Burke was not smooth. Burke apparently distrusted the young producer with the sparky personality and strange hair-piece.

So impressed was Wexler by Berns that, when he established Bang Records as an off-shoot of Atlantic, he installed Berns as a partner along with the Ertegun brothers. The new company took its name from their combined initials:- Bert (Berns), Ahmet (Ertegun), Nesuhi (Ertegun) and Gerald (Wexler). For the new label, Berns expanded his range. He branched into white rock, producing artists such as Neil Diamond and Van Morrison. Berns even discovered Jimmy Page in Britain and had plans to use the future lead guitarist of Led Zeppelin as a session musician for Bang.

As Berns's success grew, so relations with Wexler became more difficult. There was the inevitable falling-out between two individuals of firm views and strong wills. Threats of legal action followed. In December 1967, when only thirty-eight, Berns died of a sudden heart-attack in New York. Wexler did not attend the funeral of his protégé.

Many of Berns's finest soul songs were written with his partner Jerry Ragovoy. A much quieter, more conservative character, Ragovoy grew up in Philadelphia. His early story matches that of other Jewish contemporaries drawn to rhythm and blues. He was brought up on classical music. As with Leiber and with Alan Freed, the small shop was pivotal in leading the young Jewish boy into another world. After high school, Ragovoy got a job in an appliance store which also stocked gospel and rhythm records for its black customers. Again, the lower-middle-class horizons were instantly broadened, in a way that would have been impossible for a gentile suburban white, surrounded by others of the same class, faith and complexion.

Like Berns, Jerry Ragovoy started producing black singers in the pre-rock age. His first hit on the black charts was 'My Girl Awaits Me' by the Castelles in 1953. He wrote a doo-wop hit for the Majors, 'Wonderful Dream' which was a hit in the national pop charts. He wrote the song under the pseudonym Norman Meade. As he was to tell journalist Robert Meyerowitz years later, he was saving his own name for the works he planned to write one day for Broadway.[31] It was under the name of Meade that Ragovoy wrote 'Time Is On My Side' which was initially recorded by Irma Thomas but which became an international hit for the Rolling Stones.

Ragovoy, in his interview with Meyerowitz, makes no secret of preferring the original versions of his songs to Joplin's. A lot of white singers, he said, make the mistake of thinking that if you sing loudly, screaming until the veins pop out of the neck, then you're being soulful. One only has to compare Joplin's versions of her 'black' soul songs with the original recordings to feel the force of Ragovoy's point (and of Brian Ward's critique in *Just My Soul Responding*). Erma Franklin's version of 'Piece Of My Heart', just like Garnet Mimms's 'Cry Baby', has a disciplined structure, together with an intensity that comes from emotion being contained. Joplin's recordings lack this discipline.

Joplin, on meeting Ragovoy, was surprised to find a conservatively dressed man in neat jacket and slacks. She herself preferred the more flamboyant styles of the sixties' hippies. It was difficult for her to understand how a man with such a staid appearance could create such soul-

---

31. Meyerowitz, R. (1997) 'Get it while you can: Jerry Ragovoy and the ghost of Janis Joplin', *Houston Press*, August 7.

ful material. Again, stereotypes are at work: black emotionality and indiscipline is the dominant theme. The intelligence and discipline of the original recordings are overlooked. In addition, the white version is the commercial success. No-one is offering Ragovoy a million dollars to use 'Cry Baby' for a blockbuster biopic of Garnet Mimms.

Ragovoy continued producing and writing for soul acts such as Lorraine Ellison and Irma Thomas. He was working for Warner Brothers, but was not always in the forefront of their thinking. He only got to record Lorraine Ellison's version of his song 'Stay With Me' because the studio had booked a full orchestra for Frank Sinatra, who had failed to make the date. Rather than waste the cost, they called on Ragovoy. Despite the resulting recording being one of his best (and Ellison's too), the resulting sales were disappointing. The company had failed to push the record, even on the black market. In fact, this failure, it is said, persuaded Warner Brothers to give up rhythm and blues recordings specifically aimed at black audiences.

Over the years, Ragovoy continued to be an inspiration to a younger generation of Jewish soul men such as Al Kooper and Mike Butterfield. Together with Harvey Brooks, Butterfield was at one time a leading member of Joplin's backing group, the Kozmic Blues Band. Kooper describes Ragovoy as his "friend and mentor".[32] Together they produced Lorraine Ellison at Ragovoy's own studio, Hit Factory.

Ragovoy's name has never exactly become well known. His anonymity is underlined by the fact that his surname is to be commonly found spelled in two ways: 'Ragavoy' or 'Ragovoy'. The *Virgin Encyclopedia of Sixties Music* quotes a former head of Warner Broth-

32. Kooper, A. (1998) *Backstage Passes and Backstabbing Bastards*. New York: Billboard Books, p149.

ers saying, "you might not know him but he produced and wrote some of the best rhythm and blues of the sixties — and he's not black — he's a man with soul".[33]

Jerry Ragovoy was not simply a 'man with soul'. Nor should one assume that a white who can write soul music must have somehow played a trick on their ethnic background. Ragovoy, like Berns, Wexler, Shuman, Pomus, Leiber, Stoller, not to mention minor players such as Goldner, most certainly had a background. However, background is not everything. The direction forward is important: from classical music to blues; from parental aspirations of conventional careers to the uncertainties of popular music; from the European world of an older generation to the culture of black America; from economic uncertainty and the threat of prejudice to success — these men moved in similar directions.

So, again and again in the late fifties and early sixties, black singers found themselves in the studios working with Jewish writers and producers to create some of the finest popular music of that era. Yet, the harmony of that collaboration should not be exaggerated. There were arguments and tensions, as well as personal friendships and mutual respect. Above and beyond these personal individual circumstances there were deeper lines of future divergence.

It is possible that the Jewish soul networks, which produced such undeniably fine music, may have had their downside for black composers. It is said that black songwriters in the 1930s took pride in Gershwin's use of African American forms. Nevertheless, they were inhibited by his success.[34] Could something similar have occurred in the 1960s with the success of Wexler at Atlantic records? It is difficult to give a definite answer

33. Larkin, C. *Virgin Encyclopedia*, p365.
34. See, for instance, Singer, B. (1992) *Black and Blue: the life and lyrics of Andy Razaf*. New York: Schirmer Books.

but there are pointers. Networks operate in particular ways: they favour those inside, with outsiders remaining at a disadvantage.

When Wexler needed a composer or producer, it was easy to pick up the phone and cajole someone he knew well from a familiar background. He could talk the same language, use the same 'brogue' to a 'homeboy'. He might call up Pomus or Bacharach. Stuck over an incomplete song for Aretha Franklin, he brought in Goffin and King. Black composers, whom Wexler might not know so well, perhaps did not get the same calls. Sam Cooke, who was both a singer and writer, resisted invitations to work at Atlantic. He preferred the independence of a major label, RAC, which had no strength in soul music. Similarly, Ray Charles left Atlantic for ABC, where the managerial lack of interest gave Charles more control over his own music.

One thing seems clear. Black singers (and songwriters) were not taken into the business side of things. When Wexler formed Bang, he brought in 'homeboy' Berns as a partner. None of the black singers — not Aretha, nor any members of the Drifters — were so trusted. In the same vein, Leiber and Stoller went into business with Goldner, not with the singers from the Coasters, nor with Ben E. King. The black singers belonged to the studio; they were not encouraged as equal partners into the boardroom (or, rather, into the back room where the fast deals were made).

Wexler used to criticise Leonard Chess for underpaying his black artists for their classic recordings on Chess Records. Wexler was proud that his Atlantic artists were paid fair royalties and that they received the payments stipulated in the contracts. But that missed the point: why were some people doing the paying and others receiving the payments? In 1968, black radicals in the media, impatient with the politics of assimilation, hung Wexler's effigy as a protest against white ownership of the soul industry.[35] Wexler, recounting the incident,

87

protested: "As a Jew, I didn't think I identified with the underclass; I *was* the underclass".[36]

But things were no longer that simple. Perhaps they never had been: it is doubtful whether Jerry Wexler's mother would have thought herself 'underclass'. In any case, Wexler was treading a familiar 'rags-to-riches' path. A partner in a successful record company is not really 'underclass', no matter what their origins or their experiences as a victim of ethnic prejudice. Wexler would soon benefit financially when Atlantic was taken over by the huge Time/Warner group, which could trace its origins to the small studio company founded by Jack and Harry Warner. They too had started life near the bottom of the social scale, but had risen to wealth and success. Wexler's political sympathies may have been the product of his early years, but his way of life was economically leaving the underclass far behind.

Anyway, by the late sixties, pressure for independent black ownership of recording companies and studios was growing. The fragile creative alliance between Jews such as Wexler and African American soul singers — a relationship which was lived and practised rather than openly talked about — could not last. Fortunately, the recorded fruits can be played and re-played now, long after the collapse of the alliance.

---

35. Ward, *Just My Soul Responding*, p434; Guralnick, *Sweet Soul Music*, pp. 383f. Some observers have suggested that the very word 'soul' came to signify black nationalism: see, Maultsby, P.K. (1989), 'Soul music: its sociological and political significance in American popular culture', in T.E. Scheurer (ed), *American Popular Music: Readings from the Popular Press Volume II: The Age of Rock*. Bowling Green, OH: Bowling Green State University Press.
36. Wexler and Ritz, p227, emphasis in original.

The Brill Years

The Jewish soul men, discussed in the previous chapter, grew up before the rock revolution. In their formative years, they had been drawn towards African American music, whether to jazz, like Jerry Wexler, or to rhythm and blues, like Doc Pomus and Jerry Ragovoy. Together, these men helped to create the sounds of rock'n'roll. For the next generation of composers, it was different. Rock was to be their reference point. They could came straight to the world of rock after their lessons in classical music. There was no need for an intermediary stage of sneaking away to Harlem or hanging out in juke joints.

Here again, among these younger composers of rock, the Jewish tradition of popular music was continued. We find new networks — or, rather, the networks of the older generation were expanded to incorporate younger talent. Ironically, this younger generation, which grew up in the age of rock, was closely linked to the Tin Pan Alley tradition, against which rock was supposedly such a radical rebellion. The members of the younger generation were not only the spiritual heirs of Irving Berlin and other New York Jewish composers. They were also physical heirs, being based in the old Broadway territory of Tin Pan Alley.

New song-writing teams, such as Neil Sedaka and Howie Greenfield, Barry Mann and Cynthia Weil, Carole King and Gerry Goffin, Jeff Barry and Ellie Greenwich, and Bob Feldman, Jerry Goldstein and Richard Gottehrer gathered in the song-writing centre of New York. There was also Phil Spector, who was to change the sound and recording techniques of popular music. In rock mythology, these composers have been dubbed 'the Brill writers'. Their years of success — roughly from 1958 to 1963 — are sometimes called the 'Brill years'. The name comes from the Brill Building, which was the unofficial centre of old Tin Pan Alley and which became the home of this new rock-era generation.

The output of the Brill composers was phenomenal. Hit after hit owed its origins to the Brill connection. Many of these were tuneful songs of teenage love and heartbreak. The rawness of 'Hound Dog' was being replaced by a gentler sound with backing harmonies and orchestral strings. If this work was following the lead of Leiber and Stoller's productions with the Drifters, then this was no coincidence. Older hands, such as Doc Pomus, as well as Leiber and Stoller themselves, were there, guiding the new generation along.

The rock histories often ignore the fact that the majority of the Brill composers, but not all of them, were Jewish. The histories of popular music in the twenties and thirties seem to have no problem identifying the Jewish contribution to Tin Pan Alley. But in the accounts of the rock era, especially in relation to the Brill composers, there is silence. Had the names of these composers been Italian or Irish, the histories might well have identified the collective output as 'Italian music' or 'Irish sounds'. As it is, the Jewish dimension passes by largely without comment.

Although the Brill Building has gone down in rock's history as the centre of this music, there seems to be a slight confusion. The Brill Building at 1619 Broadway had been the physical centre of Tin Pan Alley since 1931. It was so named because a Morris Brill had a clothing store on the ground floor. By the mid-fifties, many of Tin Pan Alley's old guard, who were hostile to the new music, continued to have offices there. So did some of the rock publishers, such as Hill and Range, who handled songs that were written for Elvis.

However, a number of composers and publishers, especially those specialising in the new music, started hiring offices at 1650 Broadway, where the rents were cheaper. Aaron Schroeder was a case in point. As was mentioned in Chapter Three, Schroeder, along with Leiber/Stoller and Pomus/Shuman, was one of the three Jewish sources of Elvis's hits. He also composed hits for other stars such as 'Rubber Ball' for Bobby Vee. He was active in the business side, managing Gene Pitney, for whom he passed on Burt Bacharach's '24 Hours From Tulsa'. Schroeder operated out of 1650 Broadway, where his company Sea Lark was based.

Aaron Schroeder encouraged young Jewish composers such as Al Kooper, who was later to have an outstanding career as a keyboard player. While working for Schroeder, Kooper, along with two other young New York Jewish composers, Bob Brass and Irwin Levine, had a number one US hit with 'This Diamond Ring', recorded by Garry Lewis (son of the film comedian, Jerry Lewis, né Levitch). In later years, Kooper was not to be proud of this light, poppy hit.[1] Levine went on to write catchy hits for Tony Orlando and Dawn ('Knock Three Times', 'Candida', 'Tie A Yellow Ribbon' and others).

It was not Schroeder's circle, however, that was to make the name 'Brill' so famous in the rock years. In the same building was Aldon Music. This was to be the catalyst, making the Brill Building, to quote the *Virgin Encyclopedia*, the home of "conveyor-belt produced pop".[2] 1650 Broadway, rather than the old Brill Building itself, was the actual home of the conveyor belt. However, the myth of the Brill Building is significant. It conveys a continuity with the earlier years of Tin Pan Alley. In some respects the myth is correct. The tradition of New York Jewish song-writing was continued. The change of address — down and across the street — is but a minor detail.

---

1. For details of Kooper's career, see his autobiography: Kooper, A. (1999) *Backstage Passes and Backstabbing Bastards*. New York: Billboard Books.
2. Larkin, *Virgin Encyclopedia of Sixties Music*, p76.

The Brill Writers

The key figure in gathering the new Brill songwriters together was Don Kirshner, the son of a tailor from the Bronx. In 1958, at the age of twenty-one, Kirshner formed Aldon Music with his friend Al Nevins. Kirshner was not dreaming of becoming Elvis or Jerry Lee Lewis. Instead, he had some very traditional role models. He has been quoted as saying that his idols at the time were Max and Louis Dreyfuss, the founders of Chappell Music back in the early years of the twentieth century. Kirshner admired the way that the Dreyfuss brothers had moulded "the greats like Gershwin, Rodgers and Hammerstein, and Lerner and Loewe".[3] Kirshner said that he dreamt of modelling his career on Ed Marks, who started a music publishing company in the evening while selling buttons during the day.

Thus, Kirshner's imagination was shaped by the great entrepreneurs of the Jewish tradition of Tin Pan Alley. He might have taken offices in 1619 Broadway in fulfilment of his dream, but, with a bit of poetic licence and more than a little romantic self-promotion, he considered himself to belong to the Brill Building. It is a measure of Kirsher's success that his dream has been translated into legend. In the history of mass entertainment, pernickety details seem so feeble when compared with the power of myth-making.

Taking offices in the centre of Tin Pan Alley was a smart move for a young publisher, even in the rock age. The Brill Building and its offshoots attracted attention from aspiring New York songwriters, especially Jewish ones. In the Jewish communities of New York not only were the older composers legendary, but, most importantly, someone would always know someone else who worked in the music business. As Al Kooper shows in his

---

3. Szatmary, *A Time To Rock*, p70.

autobiography, the young schoolboy, playing in bands with other Jews, was just one step away from an introduction to a publisher like Aaron Schroeder. It would have been so different for a kid on a farm in Oklahoma, writing songs in his bedroom — or even for a child of Irish immigrant parents living in a different New York suburb.

Such contacts brought Kirshner his first major 'Brill' signing, just two days after he had opened his office. Apparently, the young Neil Sedaka and his friend Howie Greenfield had gone to take some songs to another publisher. Having been rejected, they called into Kirshner's office on the off-chance. They played Kirshner some of their songs, including 'Stupid Cupid' and 'Calendar Girl', both of which were to become major hits. Kirshner signed them up on the spot.

Someone must have told Sedaka and Greenfield where to take their songs and given them the confidence to do so. Sedaka had been playing in a group, the Linc-Tones. The name was taken from their school, Lincoln High School. The band, which comprised Jewish boys, played at Jewish venues in the Catskills resort. In fact, Sedaka was to meet his future wife, Leba, while playing at a club in upstate New York owned by her parents, Esther and Irving Strassberg. Much later, after several hit records and children, Leba was to act as Neil's manager.

Sedaka, having signed for Kirshner, left the Linc-Tones to concentrate on song-writing. The band was to continue, however, having a name-change to the Tokens. As the Tokens, the group achieved some measure of success, enjoying US hits during the sixties with singles such as 'Wimoweh' and 'He's In Town'. Various members had careers as songwriters and producers. But none achieved the fame of Sedaka.

Strong mothers and classical piano training are recurrent themes in the stories of rock's Jewish composers. Sedaka had won a scholarship to study the piano at Juillard School of Music. He had been selected by the great Arthur Rubinstein as one of the seven best New York high school pianists. Neil's real interest lay in pop music, not that he was discouraged by the older generation. Sedaka was to tell how he and his neighbour Howie Greenfield had got together. Howie's mother, Ella Greenfield, had been the moving figure. She had heard young Sedaka playing piano. She suggested to Howie that he and Neil should get together to write some songs, with Neil providing the music for Howie's words. So, Howie went round to Neil's house. They were about thirteen at the time. Later, of course, with several tunes in their pocket, they would be directed to the Brill Building.

Sedaka and Greenfield began working regularly for Kirshner. They were provided with a cubicle, equipped with a piano. Kirshner was soon placing Sedaka/Greenfield compositions with successful singers. 'Stupid Cupid' and 'Where The Boys Are' were hits for Connie Francis, as were several of their songs for Bobby Darin. Kirshner also sold Sedaka/Greenfield songs to Jerry Wexler at Atlantic Records, where they were recorded by rhythm and blues singers such as LaVern Baker and Clyde McPhatter.

In those days, it was common practice for composers to produce demo discs of their new songs. Publishers like Kirshner would then play these demos to established singers and their managers, hoping to interest them in recording the song properly. It dawned on Kirshner that Sedaka's demos often sounded better than the finished products of the singers who took up his songs. In consequence, Sedaka, with Kirshner's encouragement, began to make his own recordings. Unusually for a Jewish songwriter of the early rock years, he was successful.

Sedaka's style, at that time, was light, aimed at the teenage market, to which Sedaka himself belonged when he first began hit-making. A series of ten hits followed, such as 'Oh! Carol', 'Stairway To Heaven', 'Calendar Girl', 'Happy Birthday Sweet Sixteen'. Sedaka's was happy, toe-tapping music. Even 'Breaking Up Is Hard To Do', which topped the US Billboard chart, proceeds at a snappy pace.

If there was a hint of unhappiness it was temporary, liable to turn to chirpiness with the next chorus.[4]

As always in a neighbourhood network, one contact leads to another. Neil Sedaka arranged an audition for his high school friend and close neighbour, Carole Klein. Carole had been taught classical piano by her mother and had been writing her own songs from an early age. Don Kirshner was duly impressed. Because the young musician had ambitions to record, 'Klein' was anglicised to 'King'. One of Carole King's early records was 'Oh! Neil', an answer to Sedaka's hit 'Oh! Carol', which had been written with her in mind. The answer record, as so often happened, failed to make the impact of the original.

Carole had met Gerry Goffin while both were students at Queens College in New York. As Carole recounts in an interview with Paul Zollo, her own lyrics failed to do justice to the melodies that she was writing.[5] Gerry provided her with lyrics that were more than clichés. As she said, not only was Gerry capable of writing from the woman's perspective, but his words conveyed a depth and sense of pain which was unusual in many of the teen songs of the period. Predictably, their model was Leiber and Stoller. According to Carole, they were bowled over by "the idea of taking street rhythm and blues and combining it with classical music", as Leiber and Stoller had done with the Drifters and Ben E. King. After all, she stressed, both Gerry and herself had come to pop from a classical background.[6]

As in the romantic, happy-ending stories told by many of the songs of that era, Carole and Gerry not only met and made friends, but soon were husband and wife. On both sides, the parents, with the exception of Gerry's father,

---

4. In 1975, a more mature Sedaka would re-record 'Breaking Up Is Hard To Do', at a slower pace, befitting the lyrics. This version, too, was a hit in the States, going to number eight in the Billboard charts.
5. Zollo, P. (1997) *Songwriters on Songwriting*. New York: Da Capo Press, pp. 144f.
6. Zollo, p146.

tried to discourage the young couple from pursuing song-writing as a career. Carole's parents wanted her to train as a teacher. Gerry, it was hoped, would pursue his science studies in chemistry. Music was a good extra, but no substitute for professional qualifications.

The parents, however, were no match for the persuasions of Don Kirshner, who offered working facilities, an immediate weekly wage and the prospect of glory. Goffin and King turned out hit after hit for both black and white artists. They wrote 'Will You Love Me Tomorrow?' for the Shirelles, a black group from Passaic, New Jersey. Initially the group had misgivings about the song, thinking that it sounded too white.[7] The record proved to be a classic, ensuring the Shirelles lasting fame. Goffin and King also wrote 'Take Good Care Of My Baby' for the clean-teen idol, Bobby Vee.

The Drifters' song 'Up On The Roof' was a Goffin and King composition. As was mentioned in the previous chapter, Jerry Wexler commissioned the pair to write 'Natural Woman' for Aretha Franklin. Carole King herself achieved chart success with a song that had initially been intended for Bobby Vee—'It Might As Well Rain Until September'. This was a teenager's lament about being parted from her love during all of the summer months. The Beatles were to pay tribute to Goffin and King, recording 'Chains' on their 'Please Please Me' album.

One of the biggest Goffin and King songs was the dance record, 'The Loco-motion'. Personal networks, again, played a crucial role, but, in this case, it was not a neighbourhood or high school contact that mattered. Eva Boyd used to look after Carole and Gerry's young kids, while the couple worked on Broadway. They had heard her sing around the house. Apparently, they persuaded her to make the demo of a new dance song that Kirshner had

7. Gaar, G.G. (1993) *She's a Rebel: the history of women in rock and roll*. London: Blandford, p36. See also, Greig, C. (1989) *Will You Still Love Me Tomorrow?* London: Virago.

commissioned. Kirshner, on hearing the demo, decided not to give the song to any other artist. So Eva Boyd became 'Little Eva' with a number one hit record. The song would appeal to a later generation of teenagers when Kylie Minogue successfully recorded it in 1988.

Social networks paved the way to recording studio and then, to the hit parade. Carole Klein's and Gerry Goffin's path to Don Kirshner represent one sort of trajectory, whilst Eva Boyd's path typifies another set of social relations. Significantly, it was a young black girl who was hired as the child-minder by the upwardly mobile whites. Blacks tended not to hire Jewish domestics. Eva Boyd would later complain that Goffin and King received the royalties that should have come her way. For their part, Goffin and King denied this: Kirshner made all the money, they declared.[8]

Kirshner, it is said, paid his songwriters around $100 a week. For this, they had to work in tiny cubicles, aware that on the other side of the walls rival teams of writers were also competing to write the catchy number one hit. Goffin and King were not the only husband and wife team on the Kirshner payroll. There were also Barry Mann and Cynthia Weil, and Jeff Barry and Ellie Greenwich.

Barry Mann had a background in classical music and had already begun studying to become an architect by the time he was recruited by Kirshner. Cynthia Weil came to the Brill stable via a direct contact with the Jewish traditions of popular music. She had been working for Frank Loesser, composer of musicals such as *Guys and Dolls* and *The Most Happy Fella*. Originally, Mann had aspirations to be a performer. During the summers, he had worked the '*borscht* belt' in the Catskills resorts, as Sedaka had done. He even had a moderate-sized hit with the novelty song 'Who Put The Bomp'. He and Weil married in 1961 and together produced a series of hit songs. They collabo-

---

8. Zollo, p139.

rated with Leiber and Stoller to write 'On Broadway' for the Drifters. Some of their most enduring work was with Phil Spector, who will be discussed separately.

Kirshner's business expanded and he decided to set up a Los Angeles division of Aldon Music. The man he chose to head up the LA side illustrates the complex, interconnecting Jewish networks of songwriters and producers. Kirshner opted for Lou Adler, who was a songwriter, manager and record producer. Years later, Adler would work in films and theatre, gaining fame as the producer of the rock musical *Rocky Horror Show*.

Adler and his songwriting collaborator, Herb Alpert, provide an interesting exception to the sociological rule that the Jewish songwriters in the early days of rock tended to retain their surnames, while the performers discarded theirs. The pair worked with the black singer and songwriter Sam Cooke. They were influenced by Leiber and Stoller's work with the Drifters. With Cooke they aimed to create a similar combination of soulful vocals, lush strings and Latin rhythms. Lou was familiar with Latin music, having grown up in a none too affluent part of Los Angeles. The resulting Sam Cooke records, 'Wonderful World' and 'Only Sixteen' were hits in both the white pop and black R&B markets.

Adler's own name does not appear on the credits of either record as co-composer. He chose the pseudonym 'Barbara Campbell', thereby changing both ethnicity and gender. Herb Alpert, on the other hand, kept his own name, first as a songwriter and later as a performer in his own right. He became a household name in the 1960s as a trumpeter, leading his band, the Tijuana Brass, with a series of snappy hits. His *annus mirabilis* was 1966, when he had six Top 30 hits and sold over thirteen million albums. Alpert's dark appearance, together with the uniforms and sound of his band, helped to convey the impression that Herbert might have been Spanish or Mexican, rather than the younger son of Louis and Tillie Alpert.

Alpert was to found A&M Records with his friend Jerome Moss. The label became one of the most successful recording companies in the sixties, not least because of the sales of the owner's own Tijuana recordings. Alpert eventually sold A&M in 1989 for a reputed $500 million. Just to complete the circle of Jewish rock networks, the publishing side of A&M was for a time headed by the son of Alan Freed, the original impressario of rock'n'roll.

Alpert was never one of Kirshner's writing team and Adler worked at a distance. The main focus remained in New York. There, among the 'Brill' composers were Ellie Greenwich and Jeff Barry. They also wrote in collaboration with Phil Spector, in addition to working for other producers and artists. They claimed to have discovered Neil Diamond, producing his early recordings for Bert Berns on the Bang label.

Neil Diamond came from a familiar background. His parents, Akeeba and Rose Diamond were children of immigrants. His father owned a small shop selling dry goods. Neil had attended Lincoln High, Sedaka's old school. It is said that the example of Sedaka, who was two years older, acted as a spur to Diamond. Bobby Feldman, who also became a Brill songwriter, was a contemporary of Diamond's. Encouraged by his parents, Neil was writing songs as a teenager. His family had contacts with the music business. His father's friend, Murray Miller, was an agent and he knew Bert Berns. So the young Neil found his way to the Brill pop factory and to Bang's studios.

Diamond was to have considerable success both as a singer and songwriter. His 'I'm A Believer' was a success for the Monkees and later his 'Red Red Wine' was to provide the British reggae band, UB40, with their first number one. In addition, Neil Diamond followed the examples of Sedaka and King in recording his own songs, such as 'Cracklin' Rosie', 'Sweet Caroline', 'I Am... I Said' etc.

---

9. For details, see Wiseman, R. (1988) *Neil Diamond: solitary star*. London: Sidgwick and Jackson.

These successes, in the early seventies, came after the Brill years were over. Diamond's work in the seventies and eighties became increasingly glitzy, rather than rock-influenced. He seemed to straddle the worlds of pop and showbizz. His career has endured. In 1993, he released a nostalgic album *Up On The Roof: Songs From The Brill Building*. Not all the album's songs were, strictly speaking, Brill compositions, but there was a good sprinkling of Pomus and Shuman, Bacharach and David, Sedaka and Greenfield, and Goffin and King songs. The reviewer for the *All Music Guide* described the record as being sung in Diamond's "usual hammy style".

Interestingly, Diamond has felt able to incorporate overtly Jewish elements into his work, in a way that none of the other classic Brill writers did. In particular, Diamond appeared in the Hollywood re-make of *The Jazz Singer*, which was released in 1980 with Diamond playing Al Jolson, and Lawrence Olivier as his cantor father. The experience of film-making was not a happy one for Diamond, although he exempted Olivier from any blame, claiming that the old actor had acted like a *zeide* (grandfather) to him.[10]

Diamond wrote a number of songs for the soundtrack. The inevitable album included traditional religious songs such as 'Kol Nidre' and 'Adon Olom', as well as 'My Name Is Yussel'. *The Jazz Singer* proved to be Neil Diamond's biggest selling album with sales of over five million. Significantly, these Jewish songs are to be found in an overtly nostalgic work which looks back to the early days of Tin Pan Alley. Diamond was not constructing modern Jewish songs for the contemporary world.

Such overt displays of Jewish culture would have been virtually unthinkable in the late fifties and early sixties, at least for any singer with pop or rock credentials. Just how unthinkable it would have been can be

---

10. Wiseman, *Neil Diamond*, p246.

illustrated by a curious episode relating to three Brill songwriters — Feldman, Goldstein and Gottehrer. Their songs had been recorded by singers such as Bobby Vee, Dion and Freddy Cannon. In 1964, the three writers decided to try their own hand at singing as a group. They recorded several songs under the name of The Strangeloves on Berns's Bang label. One of their own songs, 'I Want Candy', became a hit. In their public performances they gave the impression that they were Australian, or even British. As Bob Feldman was to say years later "but we weren't British — we were Yiddish!"[11]

Back in the early sixties, being Yiddish was not something to be proclaimed publicly by performers. It may have been the era of freedom, but Jewish rock performers tended not to 'come out'. That was not the way to enhance sales. There is a coda to the Strangeloves' story. During the punk era, 'I Want Candy' had a new lease of life. In 1982 the song became a hit all over again, this time for Bow Wow Wow, a band assembled by Malcolm McLaren, the guru of punk and the power behind the Sex Pistols. McLaren was still then a closet Jew — but that is another story.[12]

In 1963, Kirshner sold up Aldon music and founded a new company with the aim of concentrating on music for films and television. With the growth of the hippy culture in the sixties and the emergence of psychedelic music, the simple tunes of the Brill years were sounding out-dated. Kirshner looks back on those days with pride. He speaks much as his earlier Jewish Tin Pan Alley heroes might have done: "I believe that after I'm gone, my grandchildren will be whistling these tunes... these tunes will be part of American culture". It gives him pleasure that he was able to come out of the back streets "out of my dad's

---

11. Honick, M.B (1998) 'Feldman finds home in Nashville', *American Songwriter Magazine*.
12. For details on McLaren, see Rogan, *Starmakers and Svengalis*.

tailor shop and have the ability to create an environment where this sound will be part of American and international culture forever".[13]

Phil Spector

Any account of the Brill Years in rock history must give a special place to Phil Spector. Of all the young composers associated with Don Kirshner, Spector was probably the most influential. It could be said that he changed the sound of pop, not so much through his writing, which was itself substantial, especially in collaboration with other Brill writers, but through his producing. Spector, more than anyone else, saw that the new techniques of recording could be used to produce sounds the like of which had not previously been heard.

Phil Spector was to be, in the words of Jerry Wexler, a "producer's producer".[14] He drove a firm wedge between live performance and records. Leiber and Stoller may have claimed to have been writing records, not songs. In their work with the Coasters, Leiber and Stoller produced, by careful editing and re-recording, what amounted to the perfect performance. When the band performed live, it tried to live up to the standards set in the recording studio. Spector took this a stage further — a stage which with hindsight appears quite obvious, but which at the time seemed extraordinary. Through dubbing and mixing, he aimed to produce studio sounds that could never be played live. The record was no longer, in the literal sense, a record: it did not provide a document of what the artist sounded like. The artist was to serve the recording. The record thus became the thing in itself.[15]

---

13. 'Don Kirshner and Aldon Music', *http://history-of-rock.com/kirshner.htm*.
14. Quoted in Millar, B., *The Drifters*, p66.

Harvey Philip Spector was born in the Bronx in 1940. His grandparents were Russian Jewish immigrants. Phil did not enjoy a secure childhood. His father, an unsuccessful small businessman, committed suicide in 1949, weighed down by the burden of increasing debts. Bertha Spector took her family westwards to Los Angeles, just as Jerry Leiber's widowed mother had done. In California, Bertha worked as a seamstress.

Phil was a small, weedy boy — physically a most unrock'n'roll figure. He was more Woody Allen than Elvis. While at school, he became fascinated by music, and, in particular, by the work of Leiber and Stoller. It was not surprising: he was attending the same high school as they had — Fairfax High. He was far too short and scrawny — 'too Jewish' — to be a rockstar for those days. Philip, even as a high school kid, wanted to make records, rather than perform on stage.

The inspiration for Spector's first record, made when he was eighteen, came from the inscription on his father's grave in the Beth David cemetery in Long Island. 'To know him was to love him' read the inscription. Back in Los Angeles, Spector wrote a song around the phrase. He needed a girl singer and also cash to cut a demo. He recruited Annette Kleinbard, also from Fairfax High, to sing lead vocals. Two other friends, Marshall Leib and Harvey Goldstein, were also approached. The former provided the good looks and athletic appearance that Spector so signally lacked. Goldstein contributed cash to make the recording and was promised the bass part. In the event he did not appear on the resulting record. Spector played the instruments.

---

15. For a discussion of the relations between recording and live performance in rock, see Frith, S. (1987) 'The industrialization of popular music' in J. Lull (ed.), *Popular Music and Communication*. Newbury Park, CA: Sage. See also Weinstein, D. (1991) 'The sociology of rock: an undisciplined discipline', *Theory, Culture and Society*, 8, 97-109.

With his demo in hand, Spector approached Dore Records. There he met Lou Adler. A proper recording session followed. 'Spector, Leib and Kleinbard' sound like the name of a firm of lawyers. So for the record they were given the collective name, the 'Teddy Bears'. The record was a runaway success. By the end of 1958, 'To Know Him Is To Love Him', a light, catchy, pop tune, with a repetitive chorus, stood at the top of the US Billboard chart, selling over a million copies. The inscription in the Jewish cemetery had been transmuted into the breathy words of teenage love for the whole of America. No hint of the personal tragedy and the intensity of feeling it must have provoked, is audible in the record.

The Teddy Bears' follow-up records secured only minor and diminishing successes. The act had little future.[16] Spector was looking east towards the home of Leiber and Stoller. The details of his move to New York in 1959 are unclear. Had he met Leiber and Stoller previously? Had they sent for him? Did he contact them on arriving? One thing seems clear. Phil's mother, anxious for her son's future, had wanted him to secure a job at the United Nations as a translator. Instead, he was employed by Leiber and Stoller in their offices in the Brill Building. He began hanging out at Kirshner's offices. The young Phil, even at that stage, was too egocentric to become just another staff writer. Nevertheless, as he developed his own career as a producer, he was to lean heavily on Kirshner's team of writers.

It appears that the young Spector assisted Leiber and Stoller on a number of the Drifters' recordings. He played the guitar solo for 'On Broadway'. He co-wrote 'Spanish Harlem' with Leiber for Ben E. King, a record which perfectly catches the urban mix of soul and Latin, together

---

16. Annette Kleinbard was to change her name to Carol Connors and later build a career as a singer-song-writer: see, Gaar, *She's a Rebel*, p49.

with evocative lyrics. Spector also collaborated with Doc Pomus for 'First Taste Of Love', which was to be the B-side of 'Spanish Harlem'. In fact, 'First Taste' entered the Billboard Top 100 in its own right.

The one characteristic that all observers attributed to Spector was his desire for complete control of persons and situations. Spector did not merely want to produce his own records; he wanted to be in command over the whole production. He wanted no interference of any sort from anyone else. Eventually this meant having his own recording company. In 1961, Spector founded Philles with Lester Sills, who ten years earlier had set the young Leiber and Stoller on their way, arranging their first audition with the Robins. The name Philles was a combination of 'Phil' and 'Les'. Over the next four years, Spector was to issue on Philles an extraordinary series of records that were to change the nature of pop recording.

Leiber and Stoller had combined diverse, seemingly contradictory elements into their Drifters' recordings. Always, the voice of the singer stands out above the backing arrangement. Spector wanted to throw so much more into his creations, blurring the distinction between foreground and background. Unlike Jerry Wexler at Atlantic, Spector had no wish to work with stars. He was making records, not developing the careers of singers. In fact, Spector preferred to work with malleable unknowns, especially black unknowns. There was no democracy in Spector's studio. The singer's voice was just another instrument, which was there to be used as a means of realising the producer's creative conception. It was the producer who was to be the boss — indeed the star. It was the perfect solution for the ambitious rocker, who was too unsightly for those times.

In developing his sound, Spector made special use of black New York girl groups such as the Crystals and the Ronnettes, who looked good with their short, figure-hugging skirts and big hair-dos. Actually, Spector preferred to use session singers on the actual recordings, rather than the group members themselves. Apparently, the Crystals were surprised, when touring Ohio, to discover that they had a number one song called 'He's A Rebel'. They knew nothing about the record, Spector having used the voices of the 'Blossoms' in the studio.[17]

Spector was back on the west coast, recording in Hollywood, developing an understanding with the sound engineer, Larry Levine, who was to contribute much to the development of the 'Spector sound'.[18] For the songs, he was turning to the husband/wife teams of the Brill Building. In particular, he worked with Jeff Barry and Ellie Greenwich. Together with Spector, they provided 'Da Doo Ron Ron' and 'Then He Kissed Me' for the Crystals, as well as 'Baby I Love You' and 'Be My Baby' for the Ronnettes.

In these recordings, Spector was developing his famous 'wall of sound'. Track upon track, instrument on instrument, was laid down, in order to create a total sound whose particular elements could not be distinguished. Spector was using even more unlikely combinations of instruments than Leiber and Stoller had. Against a swirling background, lead vocals or a rasping saxophone solo would emerge, only to sink back again. But all the time, whatever the murkiness of the sound, a clear, hummable tune was apparent.

Spector claimed that he went in for a "Wagnerian approach to rock and roll". He was, he said, writing "little symphonies for the kids".[19] 'Wagnerian' might be stretching matters. The symphonies, by and large, recognized the traditional structure of the pop record and lasted just under three minutes.

17. Gaar, *She's a Rebel*, pp. 45f.
18. Simon Frith in his article 'The industrialisation of popular music', published in Lull's *Popular Music and Communication*, argues that with the modern technology of recording, the studio became an instrument and the sound engineer should be seen as a musician.
19. Williams, R. (1972) *Out Of His Head: the sound of Phil Spector*. New York: Outerbridge and Lazard, pp. 81-2.

The lyrical content was traditional too: girl meets boy and her heart stands still, da doo ron ron. Few of Spector's records aspired to the lyrical beauty of Leiber's 'Spanish Harlem', as the singer contrasts his gentle, shy love with the roughness of the city. Throughout 1963, Spector devoted minute care to his special project for the year: a Christmas album, which would give old songs, such as 'Santa Claus Is Coming To Town' and 'Frosty The Snow Man', the Spector treatment. The album, released under the title *A Christmas Gift To You*, ended with a personal message from Spector himself, wishing his listeners the merriest of Christmases and thanking them "for letting us spend this Christmas with you".

This was Christmas *schmaltz* laid on thickly. Spector was following in the footsteps of Irving Berlin. The Jew was demonstrating his Americanness, not merely by participating in the national Christian holiday, but by outdoing the Christians in the celebration. Berlin wrote the biggest Christmas song; Spector produced the biggest rock Christmas record. Sometimes there can be no half measures in this sort of display, whether or not it is consciously produced. Before the Second World War, the German Jewish philosopher, Walter Benjamin, complained about the Jewish bourgeoisie, who not only had Christmas trees, but insisted on large visible ones at that.[20] *A Christmas Gift To You* was Spector's enormous, public Christmas tree.

There were two records, above all, which represented the Spector sound at its most complete and which expressed an emotional depth lacking in his much of his earlier work. In 1964, Spector signed up the Righteous Brothers, a white duo with a black soulful sound. The pair had been playing

---

20. Scholem, G. (1981) *Walter Benjamin: the story of a friendship*. New York: Schocken Books. Henry Roth, in *Left and Right* his novel about pre-war Germany, wrote about the Berlin Jews who "go on celebrating their holiest festivals in a shamefaced secrecy, but Christmas publicly, and for all to see" (Roth, H., 1999, *Left and Right*. London, Granta, p224).

the clubs with limited success. Spector turned to Mann and Weil to co-write with himself a song for the duo. The result was 'You've Lost That Lovin' Feelin'', a song that builds up from a slow, deep beginning into a distinctive climax, higher and higher, as the low voice of Bill Medley plays off the high tenor of Bobby Hatfield. All the while, the swirl of sounds — strings, chorus, tambourines, pianos — moves in and out of the background.

'You've Lost That Lovin' Feelin' broke new ground. It was longer than the average pop record, running to almost four minutes. Spector feared that the length would hamper its chances of obtaining radio play, so on the label of the record the time was printed as three minutes, five seconds. Spector, as was his style, was worrying unneccessarily. The single went on to become the most played record on US radio and television, with more than seven million plays.[21] At four minutes a play, seven million plays works out at over fifty-three complete years.

The Righteous Brothers may have been white singers, singing in a black style, but their Spector records cannot be classed as 'black' music. This was not Sam Phillips getting a white person to reproduce sounds he could hear in black music clubs. By the same token, Spector, in making the Ronnettes and Crystals records, was not simply recording 'black' sounds. Nothing like the Spector sound could be heard played in a live club, whether by black or white musicians. This music had to be created in the studio, assembled piece by piece. The black singers, when present in the studio, were doing the bidding of the producer.

The technique was also to be applied to the black singer, Tina Turner. To be more precise, it was applied to the double act, Ike and Tina Turner. Ike at that time controlled Tina's private and public life. But in the studio, Spector, as always, wanted total control himself. He made

<hr>

21. The figure comes from a BMI survey reported by Bronson F. (1997). 'You've Lost That Lovin' Feelin'' tops list of most-performed songs', *Music World*, winter.

sure that Ike was a witness, rather than a participant. Again, Spector was using an act that was not an established success. Spector produced a whole album of songs with Tina Turner, including her version of Pomus and Shuman's 'Save The Last Dance For Me'. The high spot was the song which was issued as a single; 'River Deep Mountain High', written with Barry and Greenwich. This was to be the culmination of Spector's Wagnerian progress — a perfect match of singer, song and sound, delivered with passion and encompassing climaxes, pauses and tone changes all within a few minutes.

Again, this was no simple 'black' or 'white' music. Tina Turner recalls that it was unlike the rhythm and blues that Ike had previously directed her to sing. She claimed in her autobiography that she loved 'River Deep Mountain High' because "for the first time in my life, it wasn't just R&B — it had structure, it had melody". Ike, she went on, was always asking her to scream, but Phil had said "no, no — I just want you to stick to the melody".[22]

Released in the summer of 1966, the record should have made all rival songs seem colourless by comparison. Instead, to Spector's shock, it flopped completely in the United States. It was small compensation for Spector that the record was a success in Britain. Spector never recovered. Disillusioned, he detached himself from the music business, only returning intermittently to the studio. His eccentricities, always hard to ignore, became more pronounced. He had married Ronnie Bennett, the lead singer with the Ronettes. The marriage fell apart as she complained about his increasingly irrational behaviour — principally his compulsion to control even the most trivial details of her life. Spector became a recluse.

Ike Turner had an interesting explanation for the American failure of 'River Deep'. Despite being prevented from having anything to do with the record's production,

---

22. Turner, T. and Loder, K. (1986) *I Tina*. Harmondsworth: Penguin, p122.

Ike was generous in his praise of the record's quality. Race lay at the root of the problem, he said. The R&B stations in the US wouldn't play the record because it sounded pop or white. To the white stations, Tina's voice was R&B. As Ike said, America would not accept the record because "America mixes race in it".[23] Perhaps Britain, he suggested, could judge a record on its merits, without thinking just in terms of racial categories.

Ike's explanation needs to be set in its context. A year or so earlier, black singers such as the Ronnettes and the Crystals were taking the Spector sound into both the pop (white) and R&B (black) charts. Similarly, Leiber and Stoller's work with the Drifters and the Coasters had successfully crossed the racial lines. As Brian Ward has convincingly shown in *Just My Soul Responding*, in the late fifties and early sixties young blacks were buying white rock records, and white audiences were buying black R&B. Yet, by the time 'River Deep' came out in the mid-sixties, changes were underway. Black politics was becoming radicalised. With black pride, there was an increasing feeling that African Americans should support and protect their own culture. Music had to be explicitly black to appeal to black audiences.

A moment in pop history was passing and with it, the vital role of crossing the racial divide — a role that had been performed by so many Jewish songwriters down the years. Significantly, when Kirshner sold up his interest in Aldon in 1963, the black company Motown was just beginning to take its place in the charts. The Brill Building lost its influence in pop music. Many of the songwriters had produced their best work — or at least their best-selling work — by the mid-sixties; some, most notably, were to develop later as singer-songwriters, such as Carole King, after her break-up with Gerry Goffin, and Neil Diamond. The physical and personal links with the Jewish traditions

---

23. Williams, *Out Of His Head*, p121.

of Tin Pan Alley were being loosened. As Spector had shown, much creative work was to be done in the studio. The publishers' office was becoming less of a focal point.

However, that was not the end of the Jewish story, with the Kirshner era being the final chorus of a long ballad. One more turn was to occur. Spector, in fact, was pointing forward. In many respects, he had become as famous as the acts that he was recording. It was '*Spector's*' Christmas record that was marketed: it was not identified in the catalogues by the singers. He was the target of media interest. Times were becoming right for a weedy boy — the Woody Allen stereotype — to step out from the background, to appear in public. But just at that moment, Spector himself backed away.

Rock's Jewish Intellectuals

Phil Spector need not have bothered when, in 1964, he tried to conceal the length of the Righteous Brothers' record 'You've Lost That Lovin' Feelin'. So much was changing during the sixties — fashion, politics and personal morality. This was a time when conventional restrictions were being tested in all walks of life. The Beatles and Rolling Stones altered the look, not to mention the sound, of pop stars. An extra forty-five seconds on a pop record was a small matter when put alongside all the other cultural innovations that were taking place.

'Like A Rolling Stone', issued a year after 'You've Lost That Lovin' Feelin', lasted six minutes. For anyone accustomed to hearing the two and a half minute pop song, Bob Dylan's song just seemed to go on and on, verse after mesmerising verse. Nor were the words about the standard topics of a pop song. In fact, it was not clear what the words were about. There were images, allusive snatches of stories, streams of verbal ambiguities — delivered with a menacing sneer. This was rock poetry. And it made the singles charts.

Rock now had its intellectual element. Years later, intellectuals would still be arguing over Dylan's poetic merits.[1] No-one could have pored over the hidden meanings of 'Da Doo Ron Ron'. Leiber and Stoller's playlets had

---

1. The current British poet Laureate, Andrew Motion, recently claimed that Dylan is "one of the great artists of the century": other poets disagreed with the assessment: see, for instance, Thorpe, V. 'Laureate gives the laurels to Dylan', *The Observer*, October 3, 1999.

been as clear to understand as had been the songs of the great Tin Pan Alley wordsmiths, who addressed the ordinary person, speaking directly and unpretentiously. In this regard, popular music had been democratic. Of course, the intellectuals often looked down their noses at the music of the masses. Early rock'n'roll suffered from the sneers of the college-educated, who showed their refined taste by preferring to hear classical concerts, complicated jazz or the sound of their own voices.

In the mid-1960s, the cultural climate changed. It was a time of open dissent, especially on college campuses. Those demonstrating against the Vietnam war, or experimenting with drugs, imagined that they were rejecting a whole culture. Above all, music was a central part of this rebellion. 'Protest music' became a new genre and the protest songs were sung on political demonstrations. Dylan defined the mood with his 'Times They Are A-Changin'. Elvis was no longer cool; nor were the pop hit-makers of the late fifties. With weighty issues of revolution in the air, how could da-doo-ron-ron express the serious feelings of a new age? And so the new, mass intellectual music was born. Rock poetry was, if nothing else, a reaction against the seeming triviality of rock's first era.[2]

The age demanded the appearance of authenticity. The songwriter was no longer a backstage figure, lurking behind the attractive persona of the performer. Singers were expected to express their own inner feelings, not merely to be a mouthpiece for others. The Beatles led the way, writing their own songs. At first these were simple love songs, their lyrics very much in the da-doo-ron-ron tradition of writing. But they were to develop their style, being particularly influenced by the example of Dylan.

---

2. On the acceptance of rock lyrics as poetry, see: Mosher, H.F. (1989) 'The lyrics of American pop music: a new poetry' in T.E. Scheurer (ed), *American Popular Music: Readings from the Popular Press Volume II: The Age of Rock*. Bowling Green, OH: Bowling Green State University Press.

In those changing times, weedy figures such as Phil Spector no longer needed to hide in the backrooms while the visibly beautiful strutted the stage. It was a moment for Jewish males to take to the stage — not as aggressive sex symbols — but as seemingly shy auteurs. Bob Dylan set the tone. Short, skinny, large-nosed and nervy, Dylan would never have been selected by pop managers in the fifties in order to be groomed for stardom. He was no pretty boy, nor was he a macho-hunk. He was very much from the Phil Spector schools of looks. And, if one noticed these things, he looked, and was, Jewish.

Again, the statistical proportions of ethnicity are not random. Jews were to make a significant contribution to this intellectual development of rock — not that this tends to be outwardly discussed as such. *The Virgin Encyclopedia,* for instance, comments how 'Like A Rolling Stone' changed the nature of popular music. It was not merely the stream of consciousness lyrics that were novel; the sound was unlike anything else around then. As the *Encyclopedia* says, "the sound emerged from the immortal combination of Chicago blues guitarist Michael Bloomfield, bass man Harvey Brooks and fledgling organ player Al Kooper".[3] What the Encyclopedia does not add is that all those three musicians, like the singer himself, were Jewish. The *Encyclopedia* certainly does not comment on the fact that, even in the supposedly free and easy sixties, a bass guitarist wanted to change his surname from Goldstein to Brooks.[4]

This chapter will concentrate on four Jews who played leading roles in developing rock poetry. As well as Dylan, there are Paul Simon, Leonard Cohen and Lou Reed. Other singer-songwriters could have been discussed. Randy Newman, with his crafted lyrics and cynical wit, has been influential, without necessarily attracting mass

---

3. Larkin, *Virgin Encyclopedia of Sixties Music,* p167.
4. See Kooper, *Backstage Passes and Backstabbing Bastards.*

sales. During the sixties, Phil Ochs was important as a 'protest' writer, although his songs have not maintained their popularity. Then, moving into the seventies, one finds figures like Billy Joel and Jonathan Richman. Even Neil Sedaka emerged with a more adult repertoire and several best selling albums, such as *The Tra La Days Are Over* and *Laughter In The Rain*. Often dismissed as a lightweight, Sedaka, had, in fact, a hit in the seventies about immigration, which, unusually for a popular Jewish songwriter, came near to mentioning the history of early Jewish migration to the States. 'The Immigrant' rather nostalgically contrasted the welcome given to earlier immigrants with contemporary hostility against immigration.

Of course, the selected Gang of Four is all-male. There were also important Jewish women singer-songwriters. Neil Sedaka, in recreating himself in the seventies, was following the example of another former Brill songwriter, Carole King. Her *Tapestry* album, produced by Lou Adler and released in October 1970, was one of the best-selling albums of all time. It went on to sell fifteen million copies, staying in the American album charts for over 300 weeks. King was adding mature, confessional lyrics to tuneful melodies, as well as throwing in the occasional re-working of her older material. During the seventies she recorded several other major albums, including *Rhymes And Reasons* and *Fantasy*. Alongside King, the works of Janis Ian (née Funk) or Carly Simon could also be mentioned.

In short, the Jewish tradition of popular songwriting continued during the sixties and into the seventies with a new generation, composing new sorts of songs. Not all the figures can be discussed equally. A selection has to be made. But why, one might ask, those four? Why Paul, but not Carly, Simon?

Obviously any selection must reflect personal taste. Some music appeals more than other sorts. A male writer may find himself drawn more to the lyrics of harder-edged writers such as Lou Reed than to the self-analysis of Carole King. The selection should also be based on judgements of significance. There can be little doubt as to the innovatory importance of Dylan. Paul Simon and Lou Reed are not far behind. Leonard Cohen, it is true, is more of a cult figure than a mass phenomenon. Nor is he really a rock performer in the classic mould. However, his work contains Jewish themes, often diffidently presented and sometimes partially hidden. As such, Cohen's work illustrates something more general about the position of the Jewish singer-songwriter.

The new songwriters demonstrated that nothing was beyond the range of the popular song: politics, social comment, domestic detail and general complaint could all take their place alongside the more traditional themes of love, sex and dancing. It seemed as if the singer-auteurs could reveal intimate sides of their selves. Nothing was taboo. Yet, with some exceptions, there was a huge gap. The Jewish singing auteurs avoided Jewish themes, at least directly.

At the same time, American Jewish novelists such as Philip Roth, Joseph Heller and Saul Bellow, were exploring what it meant to be Jewish and growing up in the United States. Rejection of tradition, anti-semitism and the excitement of dating gentile girls were common themes in their work. The Jewish novel was becoming popular — an accepted genre in its own right. Despite the prominence of intellectual Jewish songwriters, there was no equivalent Jewish pop song. The Jewish auteurs in rock were as silent on Jewish themes as the Hollywood moguls of the thirties had been.

Just like the Jewish songwriters of Tin Pan Alley, the intellectual songwriters were inventing or presenting themselves as Americans, even as they were criticising America. Dylan, the greatest auteur of them all, led the way. As will be seen, he displayed an ambiguous, highly charged identification with the folk traditions of America, thereby identifying with what was essentially a Christian culture.

117

Unlike the older generation, these songwriters tended not to come from the poorer parts of cities such as New York. They did not grow up in neighbourhoods where they would, as a matter of course, hear the sounds of Latino or African American music. This new generation — the generation of the rock era — tended to draw upon white American traditions of music in the way that Leiber, Pomus and Wexler had immersed themselves in African-American traditions. They were 'folk' singers, rather than 'soul men'.[5] Many of the 'protest' singers, especially Jewish protest singers, were explicitly associating themselves with the civil rights movement through their music. But this music, paradoxically, was 'whiter' than American Jewish popular music had been at any time during the century.[6]

Bob Dylan

There is no denying Bob Dylan's iconic status. His face, with its expression of worry and loneliness, became as famous as Presley's. Dylan was the Presley for middle-class whites, born just after the second world war — the figure who symbolised their era, marking it off musically from that of the previous cohort. He was the outsider, when everyone wanted to be outsiders. To fulfil the role, Dylan had to be an ambiguous outsider — the outsider playing the insider-as-outsider.

---

5. This is, of course, an oversimplification. The tradition of Jews playing and writing blues was continued, most notably with Al Kooper and Mike Bloomfield. Bloomfield recorded an album with Barry Goldberg, entitled 'Two Jews Blues'. It was not a commercial success. Kooper's band 'The Blues Project', which was a forerunner of Blood Sweat and Tears, was comprised of New York Jews. In Britain, the Jewish blues tradition continued notably with Manfred Mann (né Manfred Lubowitz) and Peter Green of Fleetwood Mac. For a recent interview with Green, reaffirming his continuing love for the blues, see 'Peter Green: slight return', *The Guitar Magazine*, August, 1999.
6. Ward, *Just My Soul Responding*, discusses how the protest singers were playing to white audiences, pp. 308f.

The tension remained through different stages of his career. He was initially known as a folk singer, eschewing the trappings of show-business and singing unaccompanied without electrified instruments. He appealed to intellectuals who set themselves above the inauthenticity and shallowness of standard pop music. Next, Dylan became the rock star with backing band and amplification, much to the horror of his folk followers.

Later, as if to emphasise his independent contrariness, Dylan moved towards country and western music, even to the extent of recording with Johnny Cash. When he did this in the early 1970s, country and western music was despised by rock's educated fans as being the music of reactionary hicks. Of course, Dylan never became a standard country and western singer. He never appeared on the Grand Old Opry with glittering suit. But he did wear a wide-brimmed cowboy hat. And he appeared in Sam Peckinpah's Western, *Pat Garrett and Billy the Kid*. A further embarrassing twist to the Dylan story came when the icon of protest emerged as a born-again Christian. Always, he seemed to be escaping from those categories which would pin him down to being one particular type of musician.

Dylan was born Robert Zimmerman in Duluth, Minnesota; the son of Abraham and Beatty Zimmerman.[7] When he was six, the family moved to Hibbing, a small town near the Canadian border, where Abraham opened a furniture and electrical appliance store. The location is significant because in his early career Dylan presented himself as the mid-Westerner, the guardian of America's threatened traditions. In Dylan's case, the traditions that he was to defend with his folk music were not those that he was receiving from his parents, who were explicitly

---

7. There is a large volume of works about Dylan. On Dylan's early life, see particularly Scaduto, A. (1996) *Bob Dylan*. London: Helter Skelter Publishing; and Heylin, C. (1992) *Dylan: behind the shades*. Harmondsworth: Penguin.

raising their two sons — Robert and his younger brother David — as Jews.

The town had a small, close-knit Jewish community. The young Robert Zimmerman was encouraged to mix socially with the other Jewish kids. But, of course, it wasn't like the big city neighbourhoods in which Leiber, Stoller, Pomus or Sedaka grew up. Unlike them, the Zimmerman family was living amongst non-Jews. An effort would have to be made to maintain Jewish contacts. The Zimmermans would have been well aware that the attitude of the long-established residents in Hibbing was not always favourable towards the Jews. At that time, Jews were still barred from the local country club.[8]

The Jewish community of Hibbing was too small to support its own rabbi. When Robert was approaching Bar Mitzvah age, a rabbi had to be brought from Brooklyn to teach him his portion of the Torah. However, it appears that the young Robert's Bar Mitzvah was a big enough event for four hundred guests to have been invited.[9]

In his high school years, Robert started listening to, and then playing, rock music. He played in high school bands, singing in the style of Little Richard and shocking the high school authorities. He was mixing with non-Jewish kids, especially those from poorer parts of town. It seems that Robert was ill at ease with his Jewish identity. He didn't want to be known as the Jewish shopkeeper's son. Anthony Scaduto, in his biography of Dylan, interviewed a girl friend from this time. She was non-Jewish and once asked Robert if he were Jewish. She recalled: "He had this funny look and didn't say anything". One of his band members then said to her, "Don't ever ask him that".[10]

Clearly, the young Robert longed to break out of this tiny Jewish world within the small world of the hick town.

---

8. Scaduto, p14.
9. Williams, P. (1994) *Bob Dylan: performing artist 1960-1973, the early years*. London: Omnibus, p5.
10. Scaduto, p14.

To do this, he recreated himself as a regular mid-Western American. This was his passport out of the mid-West. Much has been made of Dylan's changing his surname from Zimmerman. He did this well in advance of opting for a singing career, so the change was not merely a choice of stage-name. Some commentators have seen the new name as a rejection of his father and of the Jewish tradition that his father represented: the young Bob, it is said, was identifying himself with the anglo (or celtic) traditions of Dylan Thomas.[11]

However, it should not be forgotten that many Jews of Dylan's father's generation had anglicised their names as a means of fitting into the society, not as a symbol of shedding their Jewish identity. For instance, Al Kooper's father had changed his name from Kuperschmidt. Phil Spector's grandfather had the anglicisation performed for him at Ellis Island. For many Jews these changes of surname were no big deal. They were not breaking centuries of family tradition. Most of the surnames, in any case, had been acquired in the last hundred years, often imposed by the state authorities in Eastern Europe. Religious Jews would consider their real names to be their Hebrew names, which do not include family surnames.

Even so, for an American of Dylan's generation, the change from a Germanic name to an anglo name could symbolise a step from the small enclosed Jewish world to the wider world of American society. That wider society was, by its traditions and by force of numbers, an inherently Christian society. Robert Zimmerman might have been taking a predictable step when he emerged as Bob Dylan, but his parents had already helped him on the way. They had given him easily assimilable forenames: Robert Allen. He was not saddled, in the Christian northwest, with Isaac, Irving, or indeed, Abraham, like his father.

---

11. For instance, Heylin, *Dylan*.

To be sure, Jewish parents in a small town like Hibbing would not have wished their children to remain continually bounded by the small world of their adolescence. A shopkeeper like Abraham Zimmerman would be ambitious for his son to acquire qualifications and to develop a professional career. For this, the sons and the daughters would be encouraged to go away to college. The parents would hope that, away from the family home, their college children would join Jewish societies and find Jewish partners, while at the same time passing examination after glorious examination. In Dylan's case, disappointment was on its way.

Dylan seems not to have been a diligent student at the University of Minnesota in Minneapolis. Initially, he joined the Jewish fraternity, Sigma, Alpha Mu.[12] But soon he was recreating himself, denying his Jewish identity and concocting all manner of stories about his background, even claiming, most implausibly, to be the pop singer Bobby Vee.[13] He was, to quote a phrase used by a number of Scaduto's interviewees, 'travelling in disguise'.

At University, Dylan began spending an increasing amount of time in folk music circles, coming under the influence of Woodie Guthrie's music. Guthrie represented the old, left-wing tradition of protest music. His was not the sentimentality of Broadway. Guthrie spoke directly for miners and share-croppers. His songs told of the hard times of the Depression. He wore no tux and bow-tie — just checked shirt and baggy trousers. He needed no accompanying orchestra. He could make do with his own guitar. His voice was rough, like the lives of the poor. Above all, he was personifying the poor of rural and small-town America. This was not the urban poor of the Jewish ghettos, which the parents and grandparents of the Hib-

---

12. Bauldie, J. (1991) 'Bobby Zimmerman in the S.A.M.. fraternity' in J. Bauldie (ed), *Wanted Man: in search of Bob Dylan*. New York: Citadel Press.
13. Scaduto, p29.

bing Jews had known and which had produced the Tin Pan Alley music.[14]

Bob Dylan not only copied Guthrie's way of making music, but he took over his persona. He would claim to have ridden the rails like Guthrie. He adopted a thick Oklahoman accent, speaking just as Guthrie spoke. Dylan, in fact, left Minneapolis for New York, in search of Guthrie, who was by now a sick man. He visited Guthrie in hospital and made contact with the New York folk scene. The reinventions of his own identity continued. He wanted to be a child of poor rural America. If asked about his parents, he would claim to be an orphan, telling elaborate stories to disguise his origins.[15] His disguises did not fool his new friends: the stories just didn't hang together. One person, who knew Dylan from the New York period said that, behind his back, people called him "that itinerant Jewish folk singer".[16]

Dylan was not the first Jewish folk singer to take on the Guthrie persona. Ramblin' Jack Elliott, ten years Dylan's senior and well established in the folk field, had been born Elliott Adnopoz, the son of a successful Brooklyn doctor.[17] He carefully hid his origins. But occasionally they slipped out. Scaduto recounts a scene when Dylan, Elliott and others were chatting together in a folk café. Elliott let slip he was Jewish. According to the singer Dave Van Ronk, who was present, Dylan fell off his chair laughing; he rolled under the table, yelling 'Adnopoz!' over and over again. He just couldn't contain himself, laughing, yelling and rolling about the floor. Van Ronk comments:

---

14. For a discussion of Guthrie's influence on Dylan, see Riley, T. (1992) *Hard Rain: a Dylan commentary*. London: Plexus.
15. See Scaduto (1996) for details.
16. Scaduto, p44.
17. On the influence of Guthrie, see Rodnitzky, J.L. (1989) 'The mythology of Woddy Guthrie' in T.E. Scheurer (ed), *American Popular Music: Readings from the Popular Press Volume II: The Age of Rock*. Bowling Green, OH: Bowling Green State University Press. Rodnitzky points out that Guthrie's music was not 'traditional' in a simple sense. He, too, was reacting against the popular music of his day.

"We had all suspected Bobby was Jewish, and that proved it".[18]

Dylan was becoming known in folk circles as Guthrie's heir apparent. Folk-singers are in an ambiguous position. At first sight, they might appear to be deeply conservative, resurrecting the music of the past and playing it in styles that appear hopelessly outdated. However, their mission to defend the authentic cultural traditions of the poor is also an implicit criticism of the mass-produced, industrialised fashions of the present. As the pre-war cultural critic Walter Benjamin realised, in an era of change the defenders of tradition can appear to be radical — they are reacting against a capitalist ethos that demands everything to be profitably modernised.[19] The paradox is that folklorism easily slips into elitism: the masses of today, with their inauthentic music, are unfavourably contrasted with the 'genuine' masses of the past.

If Dylan were denying his Jewish origins and submerging himself in the Guthrie tradition, then he would not be able to avoid taking on the explicitly Christian aspects of this musical genre. Guthrie, in his songs, sometimes depicted Christ as a hero, a democratic friend to the poor. A tape recording of Dylan singing in 1960 contains his version of Guthrie's 'Jesus Christ', in which the Christian saviour is praised as a rebel and outlaw.[20] Being a supposed man of the rural west entailed the young Dylan singing religious songs like 'Jesus Met The Woman At The Well'.[21] He was also singing old black blues. In fact, his first known recording was to accompany the blues singer, Big Joe Williams.[22] Again, these songs often had their Christian references. Dylan's own first album, entitled simply *Bob Dylan* and released in 1961, contained folk and

---

18. Scaduto, p67.
19. Benjamin, W. (1973) *Illuminations*. London: Fontana/Collins.
20. Williams, *Bob Dylan*, p14.
21. Scaduto, p63.
22. Scaduto, pp. 95f.

blues standards, as well as Dylan's reworking of traditional music. His song 'In My Time Of Dyin" was based on Blind Willie Johnson's 'Jesus Make Up My Dyin' Bed' and Charley Patton's 'Jesus Is A Dying Bed-Maker'.[23]

For his second album, *The Freewheelin' Bob Dylan*, Dylan included some of his own material, such as 'Masters of War' and 'Blowin' In The Wind', which were to become classic anti-war protest songs. Clearly, Dylan was on the progressive side; his songs made connections with the campaigns against the Vietnam war and against segregation in the deep South. These protest songs were sung, in true folk style, to the simple accompaniment of guitar and harmonica. More protest songs came on the third album, *The Times They Are A-Changin'*, including the title song. 'A-changin" is a curious phrase with which to announce the start of a new era. Linguistically it recalls the past — maids 'a-courting' and 'a-milking'. No-one in the second half of the twentieth century was talking of things a-changing. Dylan was not Leiber, adopting the current language of the streets. He was looking backwards to past American times, even to times before the Zimmermans had arrived in the New World.

The third album also had 'North Country Blues', which, it has been said, expresses Dylan's own childhood memories from Minnesota.[24] The song is written in the first person singular. However, its 'I' is not young Robert Zimmerman. The 'I' is not only a woman, but is a long rooted native of a northern mining town. Significantly, the 'I' claims not to have parents, but is an orphan raised by her brother. The singer laments the decay of the town, where the mines are closing. All is falling apart. No jobs are left. My children will leave, the singer says. The stores are folding one by one, the singer declares in the final verse.

23. Hatch, D. and Millward, S. (1987) *From Blues to Rock: an analytical history of pop music*. Manchester: Manchester University Press, p110.
24. Heylin, *Dylan*, p5.

Thus in recreating the north country of his childhood, Dylan shifted his own identity. He writes from the perspective of the miner's family — not from the store owner's family. Dylan is not his childhood self in the song — the shopkeeper's son for whom the rabbi travelled from Brooklyn. He is one of the miners' children, with whom he would scarcely have mixed and who would not have escaped to the University of Minnesota. If 'North Country Blues' uses childhood memories — and there is every reason to think that the images of the decaying town are remembered images — then, in a sense, Dylan created a 'playlet' just as Leiber and Stoller did in their songs.

Popular Jewish song writers, from Irving Berlin and Mel Tormé down to Phil Spector, have demonstrated their universality by outdoing the Christians with their Christmas songs. An intellectual protest singer is not likely to come up with a sentimental Christmas ballad, at least sung in a straightforward way. Dylan, in his protest days certainly had no Christmas number. The protest singer's equivalent of the Christmas song is to drop the name of Jesus into songs, while keeping tell-tale signs of Jewish identity at bay.

'With God On Our Side' was also on Dylan's third album: a powerful criticism of American culture. In the first verse, the singer says that the country from which he comes is "called the Midwest". No further heritage is given. The song recalls the wars which someone from the American Midwest would have been brought up to believe had been fought in the name of God: we have fought the Indians and the Spanish — now we are learning to hate the Russians. In the penultimate verse, the singer wonders whether Jesus Christ was betrayed, or did Judas have 'God on his side'? The reference is ambiguous — but it is a Christian reference.

The little pronouns of 'we' and 'they' can act as powerful indicators of identity. Economically, the singer indicates who 'we' are and who 'we' are not. One verse of 'With God On Our Side' recounts the Second World War.

126

When the war ended, so the song goes, the Germans became 'our' friends and now they, too, have God on their side. The anger is clear. The Germans became our friends although they murdered six million — "in the ovens they fried". The song does not mention that these victims were Jewish. The pronouns are significant: 'we' are Americans, while Jews are 'they'. In this way, Dylan presents himself as a typical American (non-Jewish) Mid-Westerner. 'We' remain the Americans — even though 'we' are criticising ourselves with force. The Jew is singing as a Christian American, while criticising Christian America.

The outsider, in choosing the folk idiom, was expressing himself as an insider, while distancing himself from the sort of popular music which Jews had done so much to fashion. A radio interview given in 1966 indicates that Dylan was aware of the connections between Jews and pop music, especially that associated with the Brill Building. Dylan was criticising the folk magazine *Sing Out!*, which in turn had criticised Dylan for not being pure enough in his music. Dylan complained that "the organization and the bosses behind that magazine work in the Brill Building, in Wall Street, and... in the toothpaste company".[25] Dylan would be well aware of the magazine's editor, Irwin Silbar. Mischievously the interviewer then suggested that it was all a Jewish conspiracy; the interviewer even referred to the anti-semitic Protocols of the Elders of Zion.[26] Dylan's reaction was ambiguous. He was not outraged; neither did he disclaim the imputation. He just pointed out that the interviewer had said it, not himself.

---

25. The interview is fully transcribed in Dylan, B. (1993) *Hungry as a Racoon: Bob Dylan talks to his fans and other strangers, 1966 and 1986* (transcribed and annotated by J.B. Way), p18.
26. The Protocols were a notorious anti-semitic forgery, produced in the early twentieth century in czarist Russia. They purported to be the secret plan of the 'King of the Jews' for taking over the whole world. The Protocols had an immense impact on anti-semitic thinking, including that of the nazis. See N. Cohn, (1967). *Warrant For Genocide*. London: Chatto Heinemann.

By 1966 the folklorists had begun to turn on Dylan. The previous year, Dylan's folk phase had come to an end. Having heard the music of the Beatles, he was attracted to the idea of putting his songs to a rock backing. Not only would this allow him greater musical scope but he would be able to create contemporary 'folk' music, reaching a greater audience. Dylan's purist fans, who imagined their tastes to be a cut above the commercialism of pop, were shocked. Playing an electrified guitar was the height of immorality.

Dylan toured the UK in spring 1966 with a rock band accompaniment. In the first half of each concert, Dylan would sing his traditional songs unaccompanied, and to great applause. For the second half, he would launch into the new rock material, to be greeted by booing. In one notorious episode, the cry of 'Judas' could be clearly heard.[27] There was no irony in the accusation. A Jew was being accused of being Judas for not remaining bound to the traditions of rural Christian American folk music.

Dylan's rock music from the mid 60s is arguably among the finest of his output. Certainly, it transformed the rock song. Henceforth, rock could have lyrics which could be compared with Keats and Shelley. Professors of literature dissected Dylan's imagery and significance in ways which they have never done with Gershwin, Berlin or Pomus. Some have searched for cryptic Biblical, even caballic, allusions. No doubt they can be found, if the critic is imaginative enough. Whether they were intended by the author is another matter, for Dylan claims to write quickly with the words tumbling out, beyond his control.[28]

It is not difficult to find Jewish influences. The opening verse of 'Highway 61 Revisited' irreverently retells

---

27. For details of the episode, see Lee, C.P. (1998) *Like The Night: Bob Dylan and the road to the Manchester Free Trade Hall*. London: Helter Skelter Publishing. The cry can be heard on the Columbia CD misnamed *The Royal Albert Hall Concert*.
28. Zollo, *Songwriters on Songwriting*, p80.

the story of the binding of Isaac. God is telling Abraham to "kill me a son". Abe is replying "man you must be putting me on". The joking familiarity with God—the imagining of an argument with the Almighty—is itself very Jewish, to be found in orthodox texts and in Broadway versions of Judaism, such as *Fiddler on the Roof.* Abraham is treated with familiarity in the song: he is 'Abe', just as Dylan's father, too, was called Abe.[29]

Certainly, Dylan's interests have included religion and spirituality. The songs on *John Wesley Harding*, such as 'I Dreamed I Saw St Augustine', contain Biblical references. On this album, first released in 1967, Dylan is celebrating the old American west. John Wesley Hardin was a 'Wild West' outlaw, a Robin Hood figure, supposedly stealing from the rich to give to the poor. The album contains the revealing 'I Pity The Poor Immigrant'. The lyrics rage against 'the immigrant', who "uses all his power to do evil", "falls in love with wealth", "builds his town with blood" and so on. The sentiments are ugly. The insider is turning on the outsider. But Dylan was no insider: he was still travelling in disguise. What better way to try to convince yourself and others that you are an insider than to use the traditional images of hatred against the immigrant?[30]

During the seventies, Dylan became Christian, making records which overtly preached his new faith. Ironically, Dylan chose Jerry Wexler to be the producer of his most Christian album, *Slow Train Coming.* During the recording Dylan tried to interest Wexler in Biblical matters.

---

29. Interestingly, another song from the sixties, which includes a dialogue with God, had a Jewish author, Peter Green. Fleetwood Mac's 'Oh Well' has the singer talking to God on a familiar basis.

30. Dylan's 'I Pity the Poor Immigrant' is so different in sentiment from Sedaka's 'The Immigrant', which looks back rather rosily to the time when "strangers were welcome here" and when the "days were sweet and clear". Sedaka's song may not be great music, nor its lyrics poetic, but there is no doubting its good-hearted sentiment.

Wexler comments: "When I told him he was dealing with a confirmed sixty-three-year-old Jewish atheist, he cracked up".[31] Wexler was tolerantly amused by the whole business: "I liked the idea of Bob coming to me, the Wandering Jew, to get the Jesus feel".[32]

In his musical and spiritual quest, Dylan also seems to have been something of a Wandering Jew. He did not remain locked within born-again Christianity. He went through a Jewish phase. Scaduto suggests that he started studying Hebrew. Not one to do anything by half measures, Dylan apparently made contact with the right-wing Jewish Defense League, whose extreme Zionist nationalism was fascistic.[33] Dylan was later photographed at the Western Wall in Jerusalem, wearing *tallit* (prayer shawl) and *tephillin* (phyllacteries) on the occasion of his son's Bar Mitzvah.

The Jewish period seems to have left less direct influence on Dylan's music than his missionary Christianity. There are no Hebrew songs, or explicitly Jewish quotations, to match the overt Christianity. However, Dylan's 1983 album, *Infidels* contains an implicitly pro-Zionist song. 'Neighbourhood Bully' is a thinly veiled parable about the history of the Jews. The song describes the so-called 'bully', who has been driven out of every land. His family have been scattered; he is constantly on trial just for being born; and now, outnumbered by a million to one, he's accused of being the neighbourhood bully by pacifists who wouldn't hurt a fly, but who would let the one they call the 'neighbourhood bully' be destroyed. The song expresses themes which would have been unthinkable fifteen years earlier. Yet it still conveys its message indirectly. Neither 'Israel' nor 'Jews' are explicitly named as such. The pronoun remains the third person: it is 'he' not

---

31. Wexler and Ritz, *Rhythm and the Blues*, p15
32. Wexler and Ritz, p292.
33. Scaduto, p280.

'we' or 'I'. The song is not, it must be said, one of Dylan's best pieces.

In the twentieth century, Jewish creativity has owed much to the simultaneous power and powerlessness of the outsider. Someone comfortably placed within the American folk tradition may not have been able to transform that tradition. Such a person might reproduce folk tunes which had been handed down four-square by parents and grandparents, just as Abe and Beatty Zimmerman wanted young Robert to reproduce the traditional cantillation of his Bar Mitzvah portion. Or, just as likely, the recipient of the folk tradition might move on. The sons and daughters of Hibbing's miners no doubt preferred Elvis to Woody Guthrie, just as Robert, in common with so many American Jews of his generation, preferred the singing of Woody and Little Richard to those of his rabbi.

Dylan's music was that of an outsider posing as a dispossessed insider. He claimed an American folk tradition that had not belonged to his grandparents. In taking over this tradition, and claiming to be its guardian, he could not but subvert it. His imagination would not stand still. He had to keep moving — to keep wandering — as if fearing exposure, just as, when a young man, he had feared being revealed as 'Zimmerman'. The result has been an uncomfortable but undoubtedly genuine originality that resists easy summary.

Paul Simon

Dylan changed the very nature of popular music. He broke preconceptions about what should be the subject matter and length of a popular song. Where Dylan went, others were bound to follow. Paul Simon, for one, has said that without Dylan he would never have written the sorts of lyrics that he did. According to Simon, Dylan "made it possible for a whole group of lyricists to come onto the scene".[34]

Simon came from a middle class Jewish family in Newark, New Jersey. Like his school friend, Art Garfunkel, Paul had a fairly conventional Jewish upbringing. Paul's father was less observant than his mother. On High Holydays there would be family tension about synagogue attendance. Nevertheless, Paul had a Bar Mitzvah. Art sang in his synagogue's choir and even acted as cantor at his own Bar Mitzvah ceremony. As one biographer has commented, "both boys were well grounded in their religious heritage".[35]

Paul's father, Louis Simon, had been a professional bass player, playing in jazz bands. However, in mid-life, he switched career, becoming a professor of linguistics at City University. He still played part-time and even encouraged Paul to play with his band. When the young Paul started making music with Art Garfunkel, he was told by his mother, Belle Simon, that making music was all very fine, but "you can't make a living out of it".[36]

Paul and Art began writing their own songs. Because of his father's connections in the musical world, Paul knew where to take their songs; he started with the publishers in the Brill Building.[37] Despite a number of early rejections, Simon and Garfunkel struck lucky. In 1957, when the pair were still fifteen, they recorded one of Paul's songs 'Hey Schoolgirl'. True to the times, they did not use their own 'too Jewish' names, but were billed as 'Tom and Jerry'. The song was a top ten hit. They appeared on 'American Bandstand', on the same day as Jerry Lee Lewis sang 'Great Balls Of Fire'.

Subsequent Tom and Jerry records achieved diminish-

34. Humphries, P. (1988) *The Boy in the Bubble: a biography of Paul Simon*. London: Sidgwick and Jackson, p15.
35. Morella, J. and Barey, P. (1992) *Simon and Garfunkel: old friends*. London: Robert Hale, p8.
36. Quoted in Humphries, *The Boy in the Bubble*.
37. Morella and Barey, *Simon and Garfunkel*, p15.

ing success. Between 1958 and 1962 Paul made a number of other pop records, again recorded under pseudonyms. For 'True and False' he was 'True Taylor' and for 'Motorcycle' he appeared as Tico of 'Tico and the Triumphs'. Then he was 'Jerry Landis' with equally unsuccessful songs such as 'Cards Of Love' and 'The Lonely Teen Ranger'. Art also recorded under the pseudonym, 'Artie Garr'.

Paul and Art's interests, however, were moving away from pop and towards folk music. Art went to college, and Paul travelled to England to play in folk clubs. In England Paul started writing his own distinctive style of music, with complex lyrics that were both confessional and whimsical. In 1963, while still in England, he recorded his own song 'He Was My Brother' under the name of 'Paul Kane'. The song protested against the injustices perpetrated against blacks in the southern USA.[38]

Paul returned to the US and reunited with Garfunkel. Again they approached publishers and recording companies. The story of their signing for Columbia records is worth telling.[39] It is particularly revealing because the myth grew that 'He Was My Brother' was prompted by the death of Simon's old school friend, Andrew Goldman. Along with another Jew, Michael Schwerner, and an African American, James Chaney, Goldman had been murdered in Mississippi while engaged in the Student Nonviolent Coordinating Committee (SNCC) campaign to register black voters. The English version, it seems, was recorded before the murder. Simon, clearly shaken by the death of his friend, made changes in the lyrics for the more famous version recorded the following year. The revisions did not make any mention of the Jewish dimension.

The Columbia producer, Tom Wilson, was particularly interested in Simon and Garfunkel's demo of 'He Was My Brother'. Wilson was black and wanted to sup-

---

38. Morella and Barey, p3.
39. The information here is taken from Morella and Barey, *Simon and Garfunkel*, pp. 31ff.

port the song because of its political message. A deal was signed for the pair to record an album. During 1964, they assembled the material. The eventual songs included a number of Simon's own compositions, such as 'Bleecker Street', 'The Sounds Of Silence' and 'Wednesday Morning, 3 A.M.', as well as the revised 'He Was My Brother'. There was also 'Benedictus', which Garfunkel had adapted from an old church mass; several folk classics such as 'Go Tell It On The Mountain'; and Dylan's 'The Times They Are A-Changin''.

With the recording complete, Simon and Garfunkel still wanted to choose a name under which they could release the album. They wanted names that would not sound too Jewish, fearing lest the sales be affected by anti-Semitism. Apparently, Wilson was outraged. He criticised the pair for singing about racist injustice but being unwilling to stand up and be counted when it mattered. He insisted that they record under their own names. And so they did.

The story of how young Jews 'helped' blacks obtain their civil rights is often told. Men like Goldman and Schwerner lost their lives in the process. But there is possibly another story about how blacks helped Jews come to terms with their own identity. Wilson's insistence that Simon and Garfunkel should not hide under anglo names is part of that story.

Just three years later, when the pair had several highly successful albums to their credit, Simon seems to have glossed over the story, forgetting the original desire to use pseudonyms. By 1967 he was telling a journalist from the *New Yorker* that the pair's name, 'Simon and Garfunkel', was "honest" and hiding nothing. He said: "I always thought it was a big shock when Bob Dylan's name turned out to be Bob Zimmerman". He went on to add that "every time you drop a defence, you feel so much lighter" and that there had been times "when I've had no defences and I felt like flying".[40] He

134

did not go on to say that it had taken the power of a black producer at Columbia to insist that the defence of an anglo name be dropped. Simon was not flying so light.

Like Dylan, Simon was identifying with Anglo-Saxon folk traditions, although not necessarily those of the American mid-West. The title of the third Simon and Garfunkel record was *Parsley, Sage, Rosemary and Thyme*. The opening track was a re-working of the old English folk song 'Scarborough Fair', with more than a hint of Bach added. Simon was to widen the scope of his folk influences. The 1970 *Bridge Over Troubled Water* album had 'Cecilia', which bears traces of reggae, while 'El Condor Pasa' re-worked a traditional Peruvian folk song.

Parsley, Sage closed with its own version of the traditional Christmas song, 'Silent Night'. Garfunkel sings the song sweetly, without irony. Overlaid is a news reader, giving a bulletin. The news is all bad. Murders are described; the National Guard is to be called out because of expected trouble for a civil rights march; the latest developments in the Vietnamese war are announced. The discrepancy between the Christmas message of the song and the grim news of the bulletin is obvious. Because the song is sung in a straightforward way, with churchy, spiritual echo, the message is clear: the world is failing to match the spiritual message. It is not the spiritual message of Christmas that is being criticised.

One of Simon's most famous songs from the early period has a catchy Christian reference. 'Mrs Robinson' was used as the theme music for the film *The Graduate*. The young Dustin Hoffman played the graduate who rebels against his family's wishes for a respectable

---

40. The interview is reproduced in Luftig, S. (1997), *The Paul Simon Companion*. London: Omnibus Books, 1997: Stevenson, J. 'Simon & Garfunkel (1967)'. p5. Morella and Barey comment rather tartly on Simon's remarks.

career and marriage. The film, in traditional Hollywood style, plays down the possible Jewish references. In this regard, it is complemented by the song 'Mrs Robinson', who is assured with ambiguous irony in the catchy chorus that "Jesus loves you more than you will know".

Of all the songs that Simon and Garfunkel recorded together, 'Bridge Over Troubled Water' obtained the greatest success. Not only was their own recording a chart-topper, but there have been over two hundred recorded cover versions. The gospel influence is plain. As Simon has stated, the song has become a gospel classic, being sung regularly in churches.[41] The lyrics, however, do not contain specific Christian references.

After splitting from Garfunkel, Simon has developed his interest in 'world music', drawing on a variety of international musical sources. Latin-American influences are obvious in 'Me And Julio Down By The Schoolyard' (from *Still Crazy After All These Years,* 1975) and Jamaican ones in 'Mother And Child Reunion' (*Paul Simon*, 1971). Musicians from various American traditions played on Simon's solo records in the seventies and early eighties: i.e. Los Incas, the Oak Ridge Boys, the Dixie Hummingbirds etc.

Graceland, released in 1986, took these syntheses a stage further. Simon used a variety of African musicians to create an interplay between American and African music. Many of the musicians came from South Africa, but he also drew on musicians from other parts of Africa, not to mention the southern states of the US. Sometimes, the musicians played together in the recording studio. Sometimes tracks were laid down independently, only to be assembled later. Truly this was world music, taking rhythms, sounds, melodies and performances from different continents, weaving them together even within the same song.

---

41. Zollo, *Songwriters on Songwriting*, p97.

The title track, 'Graceland', cleverly juxtaposes the music of the American south with that of Southern Africa. The lyrics recall Elvis's Graceland home in Memphis, while the bass evokes Southern Africa. In addition, Simon added Demola Adepoju, a Nigerian pedal steel guitarist, as well as backing vocals from the Everly Brothers. The instrumental tracks were recorded in Johannesburg, the vocals in Los Angeles and the whole song was mixed together in New York.

Ladysmith Black Mambazo, the a capella church group, feature on several tracks, including 'Homeless' which combines English and Zulu lyrics. The album also includes a Zydeco track, paying tribute to the black French-speaking Louisiana accordionist, Clifton Chenier. Here, Simon used the work of the zydeco band, Good Rockin' Dopsie and the Twisters. Black South African musicians from various different musical traditions, the white penny-whistler South African Morris Goldberg, Youssou N'dour from Senegal, Linda Ronstadt from California, the Latino sounds of Los Lobos — the list could go on: all are to be found in the extraordinary mixture of the *Graceland* album.

The album was highly controversial. In the first place, the old accusation of theft was made. It was said that Simon was stealing black, African music, just as earlier Tin Pan Alley composers had stolen from African Americans. At the height of the controversy, Simon faced his critics at Howard University, a black university in Washington. The theft charge was strongly made, one angry student claiming "You're telling me the Gershwin story of South Africa! It's nothing but stealing".[42] Ray Phiri, the South African guitarist, who played on many of Graceland's tracks, strongly rejected the accusation. There was no theft, he said in an

---

42. The episode is described in Jennifer Allen's article 'The apostle of angst (1987)' which is included in Luftig, S, *The Paul Simon Companion*. See also Maren, M. 'The sins of Paul Simon (1987)' in the same volume.

interview at the time: "I think 'Graceland' is the best thing that ever happened to South African music".[43]

Probably more serious, and, in the long run more damaging, was the accusation that Simon, in making the *Graceland* record, had broken the United Nations' cultural boycott against South Africa. At the time, the UN was advocating that foreign performers, whether musical or sporting, should not play in South Africa on account of the government's racist policy of apartheid. It was unclear whether this ban on public performance technically extended to recording. If it did, then Simon was in clear breach. The argument was not pleasant. Black South Africans could be heard criticising and supporting Simon. One of South Africa's best known musicians, the exiled trumpet player, Hugh Masekela, was clear in his support.[44] Others were less positive. Some critics pointed out that neither the songs nor the record's cover notes made mention of apartheid. Others like Masekela claimed that the very music — and the fact of its black-white collaboration — was itself a living statement against racism.

Simon has continued his global experiments in his subsequent work. *The Rhythm Of The Saints*, released in 1990, took up West African, zydeco and Brazilian influences: Hugh Masekela, Milton Nascimento and C.J. Chenier, among others, appeared on this album. According to Simon, "the inspiration for the album comes from the West African drumming as it is expressed through Brazilian psalms".[45] For the musical *The Cape Man*, Simon has collaborated with the West Indian poet, Derek Walcott.

There is no doubt that Simon's world music constitutes a substantial and original oeuvre. Simon pulls on a greater

---

43. Mgxashe, M., 'A conversation with Pay Phiri' (1987), in Luftig, S., *The Paul Simon Companion*, p169.
44. See, for instance, Novicki, M.A. and Akhalwaya, A. 'An interview with Hugh Masekela (1987)' in Luftig, S., *The Paul Simon Companion*.
45. Zollo, P. 'Paul Simon — the *Songtalk* interviews, parts one and two (1990)', in Luftig, S., *The Paul Simon Companion*, p223.

variety of musical sources than ever Gershwin used in his creative syntheses. Through new recording techniques, Simon is able to mix together performances which were recorded thousands of miles apart. In this way, he can explore within a single song, the similarities and differences of popular musical styles from around the world. And all the time, the exploration is rooted, like Gershwin's innovations, in easily hummable tunes.

There is a curious gap in the musical traditions that Simon combines. African music, English folk songs, Zulu lyrics, country-and-western guitar work, Latin American rhythms, church songs, Brazilian psalms, and so on are all marked by their presence. By comparison, there is virtually no Jewish influence — no Klezmer music to complement the zydeco, nor intonations of the East European *chazan* to counterbalance the strong borrowings from the church. Garfunkel always hit the note purely and precisely, without wavering in the traditional Jewish style. 'Julio' is down by the schoolyard; it isn't Moishe or Yitzchak, who are waiting there. It is as if, in this restless travelling of the musical imagination, there is a gap at home.

Simon, it must be stressed, did not publicly deny his Jewish origins, at least after he began appearing in public under his own name. But there was a gap, even in his own knowledge of himself. His own parents, striking their own balance between assimilating as Americans and the occasional attendance at synagogue, had clearly not dwelt on past origins. In the seventies, Simon actively tried to trace his Jewish roots, hiring a genealogist to trace ancestors in Rumania: "I had no idea what I was, or even what my family's original name was".[46] He expressed pride that his grandfather was a cantor. But none of this was expressed musically in his songwriting.[47]

---

46. Cowan, P. 'Paul Simon: the Odysseus of urban melancholy (1976)' in Luftig, S., *The Paul Simon Companion*.
47. In his film, *One-Trick Pony* (1980), Paul Simon plays the part of Jonah Levin, who, like himself, is an East Coast Jewish intellectual rock singer.

Paul Zollo, who is himself a songwriter and who is Jewish, asked Simon in an interview whether his Jewishness might be connected with his song-writing. Simon dismisses the question: "I don't think there's a connection, no". Zollo persisted, mentioning that so many great songwriters are Jewish. Simon appears uncomfortable with the theme. Perhaps there is a connection, he says, "but I don't know what it is".[48] He didn't seem to want to discuss the matter further. He and Zollo, consequently, don't get to discuss the coincidence that both Simon and Dylan are Jewish. Nor do they turn to question whether the great white gospel classic of the sixties, 'Bridge Over Troubled Water' needed to be written by a Jew, just as the great Christmas song of the previous generation, 'White Christmas' had been. Simon was leaving something left unsaid.

It is as if Simon has divorced his private identity from his professional achievements. At one level he recognizes the musical tradition in which he stands. In an interview with *Newsweek* in 1975, Simon acknowledged that "it's no fluke that me, Berlin, Gerswhin and Kern are all Jewish guys from New York who look alike".[49] But, at the same time, Simon treats this common identity as if it were just a fluke. He denies that he has been influenced by the Tin Pan Alley tradition. Of all musical influences, this is the one, he says, that has had "the least effect on me". He says: "there's none of the Tin Pan Alley people that I emulate".[50] But why, of all musical traditions in popular music, should Simon claim that his own tradition has had the least effect? Again, something more is not being said.

48. Zollo, p101.
49. Quoted in Luftig, S., *The Paul Simon Companion*, p192.
50. Marsh, D. 'What do you do when you're not a kid anymore and you still want to rock and roll? (1980)', in Luftig, S., *The Paul Simon Companion*, p129.

Lou Reed

At first glance, Lou Reed and Paul Simon could hardly be more different. Simon and Garfunkel produced a pure, clean sound. There was nothing uncouth about their music or their appearance. They were the sort of boys to have delighted parents, especially Art with his blond curls and choirboy voice. Even if they sang protest songs, it was with a good liberal conscience. Who could be offended by the news bulletin superimposed on Silent Night?

Lou Reed, by contrast, oozed decadence. His dark looks, his knowing leer, suggested dangers of the night. No good-hearted liberal politics here — just seediness. And if Simon paid gracious tribute to Dylan, then Lou Reed did not hesitate to criticise the hero of the sixties' left. Dylan gets on my nerves, he said: "If you were at a party with him, I think you'd tell him to shut up".[51]

Lewis Reed was born in 1942 and grew up outside New York, in Freeport, Long Island. His father, Sydney Reed, had changed the family name from Rabinowitz and was a successful legal accountant. By all accounts, Lou had a conventional Jewish suburban childhood. He mixed with other Jewish children, whose parents had also made their way out of New York. His mother, it appears, fitted the stereotype of the dominant Jewish mother.[52]

While at Syracuse University, Lou had met the Jewish poet and short story-writer, Delmore Schwartz. The friendship was crucial in awakening his literary ambitions. At first, he had wished to write conventional pop songs. It is said that he hung around the Brill Building while working for Pickwick Records. But he was moving towards more ambitious lyrics. Whatever Reed might

51. Quoted in Wrenn, M. and Marks, G. (1993) *Lou Reed: between the lines*. London: Plexus, p23.
52. Bockris, V. (1995) *Lou Reed: the biography*. London: Vintage.

have said about Dylan, there is little doubt that Dylan had shown how rock could be combined with a poetic sensibility.

The key event in Lou Reed's musical development was the founding of the Velvet Underground with John Cale, who had been trained as a classical musician. The band became associated with Andy Warhol's 'Factory'. Its music was a strident synthesis of subtlety and crudity, driven by disturbing lyrics.

Dylan and Simon may have paid dues to the folk tradition. Reed did not. The music was electronic with a rock beat and loud, crashing discords. There was no straining after beauty à la Garfunkel. Menace was the mood, combined with an apparent disdain for popularity. This was fierce stuff, without choirboy looks to please the parents. Yet, curiously, many of the songs retained the structures of classic Brill-type pop melodies.

What distinguished Reed's songs from conventional pop songs was the lyrics. Dylan and Simon could be said to have attempted to elevate the pop song, raising it lyrically to new levels. Reed was dragging it down — further down than it had every been before. He told stories of drugs and sado-masochism. *The Velvet Underground And Nico,* which claimed to be produced by Andy Warhol, contained long songs such as 'I'm Waiting For The Man' and 'Heroin' which pitilessly told of the drug underworld: needles, pain, obsession, degradation and momentary bliss mark this world. Mikal Gilmore has written that Reed's songs with the Velvet Underground "depict a leering, gritty version of urban life that, until the Velvets, had rarely been alluded to — much less exalted — in popular music".[53]

After Velvet Underground split up — amid the usual acrimony and jealousy — Reed continued to write and perform. 'A Perfect Day' showed a gentler side. 'Walk On The

53. Gilmore, M. (1999). *Night Beat*. London: Picador: p105.

Wild Side', which has become a rock classic, again depicted street life. It told the stories of sexual transgressives and hustling prostitutes. Reed was not moralising. Rather he was celebrating the spirit of street-life and the various addictions of its inhabitants.

There has been much confusion about whether Reed was singing about himself. He has compared his songs with novels, denying that he identifies with the characters about whom he sings. The novelist's first person singular can be a created character, and so can the songwriter's 'I'. When Reed sings 'I'm Waiting For The Man', he is not necessarily singing of himself. But nor is he distancing himself from that 'I'.

As one might expect, there are few religious allusions in Reed's vision: he is not peddling spirituality, whether Jewish, Christian or otherwise. In 'Heroin', he might say that he feels like the son of God. No-one could mistake this description of drug-induced ecstasy for religious preaching. If anything, it is anti-religious, reducing the spiritual to the sordid. Reed's later *New York* album, however, criticises Jesse Jackson and Louis Farrakhan for anti-semitism. But that's about it, except for a remark quoted by his biographers. When asked whether he was Jewish, Reed is said to have replied "of course I'm Jewish, aren't all the best people?"[54] It's a good throwaway line — and it is one that stops the interviewer from taking his questions down that particular path.

If one is looking for a precedent for Reed's work, then perhaps it should be Kurt Weill, the Jewish composer who looked at pre-war Germany with a shocking directness. Weill (yet another son of a cantor), however, had a political vision. In particular, his work with Bertold Brecht expressed a Marxist optimism for the future. Reed, by contrast, dispenses with politics. He is not preaching a message, just describing and relishing the dangerous world of city streets.

---

54. Quoted in Wrenn and Marks, *Lou Reed*, p10.

Yet, another connection can be made. Reed's vision of urban life can be compared with the playlets of Leiber and Stoller. At first glance, the comparison seems absurd. Leiber and Stoller provide jokey, snappy glimpses, shot through with optimism; Reed's work does not flinch from darkness and despair. But Reed was following Leiber and Stoller in writing urban 'playlets'. He claims that "one of my strong points is that I'm good at dialogue...it's a sort of polished version of the way people speak" — just like, for instance, Leiber and Stoller's 'Yakety Yak'.[55] This differs from Dylan's stream of poetic consciousness or Simon's carefully constructed imagery.

It is possible to make a further connection between the happy, melodious sounds of the Drifters and the dark, intellectual melancholy of the Velvets. Both were making music of the city; both know that the city offers suffering and pleasure. Melancholy is detectable even in The Drifters' summer vacation song, 'Under The Boardwalk'. It was recorded the day after the band's lead singer was found dead of a drug overdose. The studio had already been booked and the recording company would not permit the cost of a postponement. One of the other singers in the group had to step up to take the solo. This is a world that Reed understood.

There is, however, a difference between Reed's songs and those of Leiber and Stoller. The latter were writing for black singers, using black phrasing to do so. Reed's words are written principally for himself to sing. And sometimes they identify the singer as white. The pusher, for whom the singer waits in 'I'm Waiting For The Man', is conveyed as black: the singer recounts how the 'man' calls him 'white boy'.

In an important respect, Reed shares the outlook of Leiber and Stoller, as well as that of Doc Pomus. He does not censor outcasts. In 'Coney Island Baby', he tells us that the city is a "funny place" and he reminds us that people have

---

55. Reed quoted in Wrenn and Marks, *Lou Reed*, p. 17. Also, Doggett P. (1991) *Growing up in public*. London: Omnibus, p14.

"peculiar tastes". The song is about the "glory of love". Reed's instincts are to include, not exclude: no-one, not even the meanest hustler nor those branded as perverted by the mainstream, should be denied the possibility of love.

Lou Reed, unlike the younger Dylan, did not distance himself from the pop music of the early sixties. He had tried his hand as a pop songwriter. Reed and Doc Pomus became close friends. During Pomus's last weeks in hospital, Reed visited him virtually everyday. After Pomus's death, Reed said that "not a day goes by when I'm not painfully aware that I can't just pick up the phone and call him". He added "I really loved Doc".

To love the man, Reed loved the man's music. Pomus's family arranged for a tribute album to be made in the great songwriter's memory. Dylan contributed, giving an amazingly good version of 'Boogie Woogie Country Girl' — the Pomus song which Big Joe Turner had originally recorded. Reed, too, sang on the album. For his contribution, Reed chose 'This Magic Moment', which Pomus had written for the Drifters. The way Reed sings the song, he could have written it himself.

Leonard Cohen

The last of the four singer-songwriters, Leonard Cohen, differs from the other three. In the first place, he is older than the others, having been born in 1934. He is Canadian, rather than American. His background is in the literary world, rather than that of rock or folk music. The beat of rock'n'roll has little place in Cohen's music. Even unquestioned admirers admit that Cohen's songs often seem to proceed at a "rather laboured, not to say funereal pace".[56] And lastly, in contrast to Dylan,

---

56. Dorman, L.S. and Rawlins, C.L. (1990) *Leonard Cohen: prophet of the heart*. London: Omnibus, p216. Dorman and Rawlins provide an excellent account of the Jewish influences on Leonard Cohen's life.

Simon and Reed, Cohen grew up securely within, and has remained firmly rooted to, the religious traditions of Judaism even when supplementing them with Zen Buddhism.

Leonard Cohen did not start issuing records until he was well into his thirties. Already he had a track record of publishing the printed word. Dylan, Simon and Reed have all been compared with poets, although literary critics have disputed whether their lyrics really constitute proper poetry. In the case of Cohen there can be less dispute. In a literal sense, he is a poet: he published several volumes of poetry before he took to making records. Critics may judge some of the stuff to be poor poetry, but they would not deny its status as poetry. Some of Cohen's songs were first published as poems and only later did Cohen set them to music. After he became famous for his records, his poetry books, which formerly had only attracted the tiny sales typical of poetry, sold in vast quantities. Cohen also published a couple of novels, one of which, *The Favourite Game*, is semi-autobiographical.[57]

Cohen has not made hit singles. He is not to be found in mega-stadiums with dry ice and laser lights. He wears sombre suits. His gloomy voice is matched by mournful melodies. He has always looked too mature to be involved in the silliness of the popular music business. In the late sixties, his records were played in thousands upon thousands of student bed-sits. He has continued to record. The later work has become more Jewish in its points of reference. Cohen has called this later work "Jewish blues".[58] But, as will be seen, his Jewish blues are neither written nor sung in a straightforward way.

Cohen was brought up in Montreal, where his father's family were prominent, long-established members of the Jewish community. His grandfather, a successful businessman, had been president of the main Montreal syna-

---

57. Cohen, L. (1970) *The Favourite Game*. London: Secker and Warburg.
58. Quoted in Dorman and Rawlins, p181.

gogue, and had been active in community affairs both within and outside Jewish circles. His sons, including Leonard's father, carried on the good work, attending synagogue regularly and occupying seats reserved for the important members of the congregation.

The Cohens seem to have typified the respectability of 'Anglo-Judaism', in which Jewish tradition is combined with British-style manners and polite behaviour. The resulting synthesis is more orderly and formal than East European shtetl Judaism. Leonard's mother, by contrast, had been born in Poland and had fled from persecution. She was descended from a line of rabbis. Yiddish was her first language and she sang Yiddish songs to the young Leonard. Within the Montreal Jewish community, she had felt herself to be a social rank beneath the Cohens. Her warmer, more emotional, mystical tradition of Judaism was not quite the way of the Montreal Cohens.

Leonard had the sort of Jewish education that one would expect for a boy from such a bourgeois, deeply Jewish family. He attended *cheder* (Hebrew religion school) three times a week, studying Hebrew and the holy texts. In 1943, when Leonard was still a boy, his father died. The masculine responsibilities of traditional religious practice, both in the home and in the synagogue, fell on his shoulders.

Neither as an adolescent nor later as a university student, did Leonard try to throw off his Judaism. There was no travelling in disguise. He still kept up ritual practices, although at times he might have disputed the principles of Jewish philosophy.[59] When he became interested in poetry, his chief guides were both Jewish: Irving Layton, the poet, and Louis Dudeck, his tutor at McGill University. Layton and Dudek were both concerned to express in

59. Nadel, I.B. (1996) *Various Positions: a life of Leonard Cohen*. London: Bloomsbury, p19.

their respective writings, Jewish sensibility within a Canadian context.[60]

Their influence can be seen in Cohen's early poetry, which openly explored Jewish themes. His first book of poems, *Let Us Compare Mythologies*, appeared in 1965 and was dedicated to the memory of his father.[61] 'Lovers', for example, was about the Holocaust and 'Prayer for Messiah' used Jewish imagery. His next volume was *The Spice-Box of Earth*, which was published in 1961. The book was dedicated to the memory of his mother's father, Rabbi Klein, and to his paternal grandmother. The title of the book refers to the Jewish ritual object which is used to mark the end of the Sabbath. Even more than the first book, *Spice-Box* combined a sense of Jewish spirituality with sensuousness. Delight in the Sabbath, and regret for its transience, are expressed in poems such as 'After The Sabbath Prayers' and 'Song For Abraham Klein'. In 'Last Dance At The Four Penny' he paid tribute to his friend Irving Layton, sharing the latter's irreverent celebration of Judaism: "Who cares whether or not the Messiah is a Litvak?" the poem asks.[62]

Throughout his life, Leonard Cohen has kept in touch with his Jewish roots in one way or another. He has studied Torah and Talmud at various times, and has lived briefly in Israel. Even while becoming seriously interested in Zen meditation, Cohen has seen no contradiction in continuing to pray in Hebrew and lighting Sabbath candles. His poetry, and indeed his music, might mix sexuality and spirituality. But this is in keeping with the Jewish tradition. Not only can the same mixture be found in the *Song Of Songs,* but the great

---

60. See Dorman and Rawlins, *Leonard Cohen*, for discussions of the influence of Layton and Dudeck.
61. Cohen, L. (1965) *Let Us Compare Mythologies*. Toronto: Contact Press.
62. Cohen, L. (1965) *The Spice-Box of Earth*. New York: Viking, p73.

Mediaeval poet Yehuda HaLevi combined mysticism, biblical reference and eroticism.[63]

In short, Leonard Cohen can be seen as a very Jewish author. He has not been one of Lou Reed's street types, nor has he sought to become a born-again Christian like Dylan. His Jewish blues do not involve singing Christian songs such as 'Silent Night'. When Paul Zollo put to Leonard Cohen the same question that he had put to Paul Simon, Cohen did not dismiss the idea that his songwriting had been influenced by his Jewishness. He said it was hard to estimate the effect because he had never been anything else but Jewish: "So I don't know what it would be like not to have this reference".[64]

When Cohen became a public performer he did not anglicise his name. He was already a published author under his own name. He had an additional reason not to change his surname. The idea of disavowing Jewish tradition in search of popularity would have seemed an act of betrayal. According to Loranne Dorman and Clive Rawlins in their biography of Cohen, he sets great spiritual store in being a *cohen*, a member of the priestly tribe reputedly descended from Aaron. To have abandoned the name 'Cohen', would therefore have been a double treachery.

With all this sense of rootedness, together with a strong spiritual dimension, one would expect Cohen's songs to be shot through with Jewishness. However, there is a marked difference between Cohen's written work and his songs. The books and the poetry are unambiguously Jewish. The novel, *The Favourite Game*, expresses Jewish themes without inhibition. Readers could not miss the fact that the author is Jewish. Similarly, it would take an especially obtuse reader of *The Spice-Box* to think that its author were Christian. By contrast, Cohen's records can be

---

63. See, for instance, HaLevi, Y. (1924), *Selected Poems*. Philadelphia: the Jewish Publication Society of America.
64. Zollo, *Songwriters on Songwriting*, p342.

enjoyed, even loved, without the listener catching the echoes of Jewish references.

Cohen's early songs — those that were played in the sixties bed-sits as the joss-sticks burnt and the joints were passed — have their share of Christian references. 'Suzanne', written in 1966, was inspired by a friend who lived on the waterfront in Montreal near the sailor's church. The second verse starts with Jesus being a sailor, walking upon the water. You want to be with him, sings Cohen, for Jesus has touched your perfect body with his mind.

The reference is ambiguous, rather like Simon's references. Cohen is not preaching as Dylan was on his born-again Christian albums. The singer is not trying to get the audience to believe in the Christian Jesus. If Jesus is a sailor, then he may be just a man, not a divine figure. But the reference, in a sense, functions like the Jewish Christmas tree which is visible from the road (or like the popular songwriter's Christmas song). The Christian need not feel alien. 'Suzanne' does not contain specifically Jewish images. It mentions "tea and oranges", but not spice boxes. Certainly, its verses contain no Litvak Messiah.

In 1977 Leonard Cohen made a record with Phil Spector, who was tempted out of his semi-retirement for the purpose. The songs on *Death Of A Ladies' Man* are credited to both Cohen and Spector. The result was not wholly satisfactory, as Spector's production somewhat swamps Cohen's voice. Some critics, however, have been impressed by the album's distinctive character.[65] 'Don't Go Home With Your Hard-On' deals wittily and concisely with some of the themes of Philip Roth's *Portnoy's Complaint*: boyhood erections, masturbation, the narrow lives of parents. Roth's novel was clearly set in a Jewish context, as was Cohen's *The Favourite Game*, which also dealt with sex

---

65. *Billboard* called the album a "brilliant collage of vividly lyrical paintings" (Nov. 19, 1977).

and adolescence in a Jewish home. 'Don't Go Home With Your Hard-On', by contrast, has no markers of ethnic identity. Interestingly, the song has two other notable Jews joining in the raucous, singalong chorus: Bob Dylan and the Jewish 'beat poet' Allen Ginsberg.

Cohen, in his book *Death of A Lady's Man*, published in 1978, writes of his failed marriage and his desire for a Jewish life — how he wanted the "oil lamps, order, the set table" and "the Sabbath observed".[66] In the record of almost the same name, issued the previous year, there are no such references. The themes of love and personal loss are evident, but the spiritual side is more abstractly expressed.

In his later records issued during the eighties, Cohen produced some very Jewish songs — his Jewish blues. Nevertheless, the Jewish themes are still discreetly, even ambiguously, introduced. In fact, the listener has to know the references in the first place, in order to recognize them. Like the earlier 'Who By Fire', the song 'If It Be Thy Will', on Cohen's 1984 album *Various Positions*, takes its title from a Hebrew prayer. It remains in the form of a prayer, although it can also be understood as being spoken to another person. No Hebrew words from the original prayers are reproduced in the songs.

'Dance Me To The End Of Love', also on *Various Positions*, uses imagery that could have been taken from a Chagall picture of *shtetl* life: the violin, the dove, the wedding. The tune recaptures the rhythms of Eastern European Jewish songs. There are biblical references to Babylon and the tent of shelter. On the same album is 'Hallelujah' which refers to David and to the injunction against taking the Name in vain. David, as a writer of songs and lover of women, is a figure with whom Cohen can easily identify himself. Cohen sings 'Hallelujah'

---

66. Cohen, L. (1993) 'This marriage' in *Stranger Music: selected poems and songs*. London: Jonathan Cape, p235. *Death Of A Lady's Man* was originally published by McClelland and Stewart.

accented in the Hebrew way, with the stress on the third syllable. His tune echoes traditional Jewish liturgy. The song ends with Cohen declaring that he will stand before the "Lord of Song" with nothing on his tongue but "Hallelujah". However, Cohen does not sing with the traditional waverings of the East European cantor. Then again, that was not in his boyhood tradition, at least on his father's side. Apparently, his grandfather was famous in Montreal Jewish circles for stipulating when appointing cantors to the synagogue that "You must be able to sing; but don't you dare!".[67]

In none of the Jewish blues on *Various Positions* are there any Christian references. Yet, the Jewish references are covered in such a tapestry of allusion that a non-Jew could easily miss them. The words 'Jew' or 'Jewish' are not used. The only Hebrew word is 'Hallelujah', which is so familiar in Christian prayers that it has ceased to be a Hebrew word. In private, Cohen may pray in Hebrew, but when his prayers are reproduced in his songs, English is the language. Christians need not feel uncomfortably excluded.

Some of Cohen's comments suggest that this is not a coincidence and that certain inhibitions remain about being too Jewish in public. According to Nadel's biography of Cohen, the song 'I Can't Forget', on the 1988 album *I'm Your Man,* was originally entitled 'Out Of Egypt'. Its explicit topic was the Exodus of the Children of Israel. Cohen recounted that, once in the studio, he could not sing it. The song was re-titled and altered, becoming a wry observation about ageing and desire.

Cohen has maintained intermittent contact with Israel. In 1972 he volunteered to serve in the Israeli army and was appointed to the support services.[68] His military experiences were to find their way into song in 'Field Commander Cohen'.[69] The song is obscure. There is no actual

---

67. Dorman and Rawlins, p12.
68. Dorman and Rawlins, p260.
69. Nadel, p199.

mention of Israel or military service. It is hard to know what the song is about. As Dorman and Rawlins comment, "'Field Commander Cohen' has been described as one of the most incomprehensible of Leonard's songs".[70] It is as if its subject matter cannot be dealt with head-on.

In his interview with Paul Zollo, Cohen mentioned that his original version of 'Democracy' dealt with the relations between blacks and Jews. The 'J' word, 'Jews', was there and so was the first person plural of identification: "First we killed the Lord and then we stole the blues".[71] When the song was issued on the 1992 album *The Future*, Cohen did not use that verse, nor other preliminary verses that covered the same topic. On the same album, the 'Future' has the line "I'm the little Jew who wrote the Bible". Zollo asked Cohen about that line and how rarely he, or any other Jewish songwriter, mentions being Jewish in a song. Cohen said he smiled when he wrote that particular line. He added that a friend had said "I dare you to leave that line in".[72]

'Dare' is a strange, but natural, word to use. There is no physical risk involved in using the line. No attack will result. Does the singer really expect the audience to turn *en masse* against Cohen because he and his words are too Jewish? Those days belong to another time. Yet, the inhibition remains. The public world of popular song can be marked by overt Christian references but the Jewish ones are, at most, so discreet that they can be missed.

If daring is required for the Jew to stand as himself or herself in the world of popular music, then Cohen has shown it. The concerts on his first European tour began with the Yiddish song 'Un As Der Rebbe Singt' ('As the Rabbi Sings').[73] But, if Cohen wished to signal his Jewishness, he used a foreign language and a song written by

70. Dorman and Rawlins, p274.
71. Zollo, p336.
72. Zollo, p341.
73. Dorman and Rawlins, p184.

another. He does not put his own overtly Jewish poems to music. The Jewish blues cannot be too obviously Jewish.

But slowly there has been a thawing. The old WASPish domination is weakening. A bit more Jewish daring becomes possible. The album *Cohen Live*, includes a version of 'I'm Your Man' taken from a concert given in Toronto in 1993. Cohen changes the words slightly. Instead of singing straightforwardly "if you want a doctor", he adds a single word to make a joke: "If you want a Jewish doctor..." A small cheer went up from part of the audience. It was a reward for daring to break out of the self-imposed inhibition, even in the form of a joke from this most serious of singers.

Paul Simon can use Spanish, Zulu or Cajun French in his works. The rock composers such as Leiber and Stoller or Doc Pomus write comfortably with adopted black slang. Dylan has his Oklahoma accent. But no Hebrew — or, perish the thought, Yiddish — slips out, at least, not in moments for recording.

Yiddish phrases are permissible in other contexts. As Cohen shows, the written medium differs from the immediacy of song. Jerry Wexler's autobiography is revealing in this respect. He is upfront about his Jewishness. He presents himself in print as a man who would use the occasional Yiddish word in conversation. He describes his mentor, Paul Ackermann, as a *tzaddik*.[74] He says that by the time he left the army he was "almost a *mensch*".[75] And so on. There is no embarrassment in using such words in print, at least by the 1990s. But none would slip into the songs he wrote or commissioned from Jewish writers.

A number of yiddish expressions (such as *mensch* or *chutzpah*) have entered standard American English. As such, they are no longer the sole property of Jewish speakers. The high art of Jewish novelists, such as Roth and Heller, has been important in this linguistic expansion of

74. Wexler and Ritz, *Rhythm and the Blues*, p59
75. Wexler and Ritz, p49.

the English language. By contrast, popular music has contributed virtually nothing, despite the fact that the words of Jewish lyricists constantly reach the ears of millions. The intellectual singer-songwriters and the early rock composers have been at one on this.

Golden Past, Silver Present?

7

A comment by the American rock critic, Mikal Gilmore, shows by implication just how enormous the Jewish contribution to rock has been. According to Gilmore, "Bob Dylan was — next to Elvis Presley — the clearest shot at an individual cultural hero that rock & roll ever produced".[1] The two heroes are revealing. Dylan is a Jew, certainly by birth. Much of Elvis's best music was written by Jews. Without that music, Elvis would hardly have been a cultural icon. The Jewish contribution, of course, does not stop at Dylan and Elvis's writers. The contribution of American Jews — whether the Jewish soul-men, the writers of the Brill era, or the intellectual singer-songwriters — has been out of all proportion to the numbers of Jews in the population at large.

Suffice it to say that the established Jewish tradition of popular songwriting continued well into the age of rock. This has not been a superficial continuity. In the case of the Brill writers, as has been shown, there was a direct physical link with the Brill Building itself. There has been continuity, too, in the ways of creating popular music. Bob Dylan and Paul Simon do not stand outside the tradition of Gershwin and fellow Tin Pan Alley composers, who developed a new American music, by synthesising musical traditions. They did this by immersing themselves in heritages that were not their own.

Thus, Arlen and Gershwin used the music of African Americans, combining it with European influences. Leiber

---

1. Gilmore, M. (1999) *Night Beat*. London: Picador, p52.

and Stoller, as well as Wexler, followed this example in a new era of popular music. Dylan attached himself to the American white folk tradition, rather than to black blues. But he did not leave folk music as it was. He combined it with rock, and then with country and western, breaking supposed rules of taste on the way. Paul Simon sampled even more widely. Using modern technologies of recording, travel and communication, he was able to combine musicians from around the world. Language, rhythms and styles of musicianship switched seamlessly in his *Graceland* album, even within the same song. As with Gershwin, the whole transcended its individual parts.

The strength of the Jewish influence in pop music has, nevertheless, waned in the last twenty years. This partly reflects general trends within the music business, which themselves are a product of wider social and economic forces. In addition, this waning is the consequence of the changing position of Jews within the United States.

The popular music industry has been dramatically transformed since the heyday of rock'n'roll. The sociologist of music, Simon Frith, dates the rock era from 1956 to 1976, with a peak in 1967. In the 1980s, rock died, Frith suggests. Nowadays there are "scattered 'taste markets'", rather than a general audience: "No single pop taste, no particular rock fragment, seems any weightier, any *truer* than any other".[2] And rock, once the music of rebellion, is used by advertisers to sell products.

Early signs of pop music's fragmentation were visible even during the period that Frith identifies as the peak of rock. As is typical in the United States, the first fissures appeared along racial lines. By the mid sixties, black and white tastes in popular music were once again diverging after a brief period of convergence. The intellectual singer-songwriters found themselves singing to predominantly

---

2. Frith, S. (1988) *Music for Pleasure*. Cambridge: Polity Press, p. 5 (emphasis in original).

white audiences, particularly to college-educated audiences. Just a couple or so years earlier, the Jewish soul men and the Brill writers had sought, and achieved, a general audience that crossed the racial divide.[3] Like Arlen, Gershwin and Berlin before them, they were not 'niche marketing' their products. They were attempting to address the common man and woman directly, regardless of race, class and creed (but not age).

It has been a continuing theme in the history of American popular music that Jewish composers, above all, have been successful in this task of creating a common music. They have been able to extract themselves from their particular position in society, in order to articulate the feelings of millions. However, with the fragmentation of popular music into separately marketable types, this task of reaching out to a common audience has, in effect, come to an end. Nowadays different types of music are aimed at different segments of the market.

In any case, the conditions for American Jewry were changing. Singer-songwriters such as Bob Dylan and Paul Simon belonged to the last generation of American Jews with older family members who had come from Eastern Europe at the turn of the century. That generation could hear at first hand about the times when anti-semitism was a daily threat. Parents and grandparents will have told them of their own experiences, passing on their own sense of distrust. They too will have caught the tail end of anti-semitism's long history.

A story told by the singer-songwriter, Randy Newman, illustrates the conditions of his generation.[4] Newman was born in 1943. He grew up in comfortable, seemingly well-assimilated surroundings in Los Angeles. His uncle was a successful Hollywood composer. When Randy was about eight, he made an arrangement to meet a schoolfriend at a

---

3. See Ward, *Just My Soul Responding* for details.
4. Ronson, J. (1999) 'Little big man', *Guardian Weekend*, July 31.

country club, of which the young girl's family were members. The girl's father then phoned Randy to cancel the arrangement, because the club did not admit Jews. The young Randy thanked his friend's father, put the phone down and then ran to his own father asking "Hey dad? What's a Jew?" ·

With such childhood experiences, it is hardly surprising that Newman, and those of his background, grew up viewing the world obliquely. By contrast, young American Jews are unlikely to encounter such prejudices today. Middle-class Jews have entered mainstream America. Their friends' parents will make no such phone calls about exclusive clubs. The young may hear about the exploits of great-grandparents who arrived penniless at Ellis Island, but these will be ancestral tales, rather than stories told by living relatives. The young may fear the activities of racist fanatics, but they will not assume that ordinary respectable citizens will discriminate against them.

Moreover, the physical conditions of life that favoured musical creativity have changed. Young Jews today are likely to live in comfortable suburbia. They are not growing up in the poorer parts of cities, like Gershwin, Wexler or Leiber, hearing the excitingly different sounds of black and Latino music coming from cafés down the street. Suburbia provides no special advantages in this respect. In short, American Jewry, over three generations, has made the successful passage from strange, foreign migrants to assimilated citizenry. For the fourth generation there is a musical loss. As Greil Marcus has written in his book *Mystery Train*, complete assimilation is musically a dead end — the novel perspective of the immigrant is gone.[5]

The younger generation of today have less compulsion to pretend, to change their names, to fear the Yiddish intonation slipping out at an inopportune moment. They may

---

5. Marcus, G. (1994) *Mystery Train*. Harmondsworth: Penguin, pp. 123f.

even revert to the exotic names of great-grandparents. In today's climate, ethnic identity can be proudly proclaimed. Cinemas will show Woody Allen acting in a way that would have made the Hollywood early moguls squirm. A good-looking star can even be called Jeff Goldblum.

Even in the world of rock, there has been change. There is less pressure these days for Jewish vocalists and band members to anglicise their names. Indeed, there is an American band enjoying moderate success today with a name that no ambitious rock musicians would have used in the fifties or sixties — 'the Silver Jews'. In a previous generation, only a band which aspired to nothing more than playing before Jewish audiences in the Catskills, would have adopted such a name. No-one else would have chosen to venture out into the gentile world with a such self-selected handicap.[6]

The Silver Jews have developed from playing punk to a softer, almost country-influenced, music. David Berman, the band's leader, writes allusive lyrics that have been compared with Dylan's. Certainly, his vocal delivery contains more than an echo of Lou Reed. He is the only Jewish member of the band. In an interview with the journalist Amy Sohn, he has talked about the band's choice of name. He comments that the word 'Jew' "should be a beautiful word", but in the past Jews themselves have had problems with it: "if you use the wrong tone of voice, it's a slur". However, Berman continued, "it shouldn't be that way". He was interested "in cutting off the associative baggage around it".[7]

---

6. There is always an exception to every generalisation. In the 1970s, the satirical country singer, Kinky Friedman, named his backing group 'The Texas Jewboys'. Friedman, both Jewish and Texan, wrote and recorded songs such as 'They Ain't Making Jews Like Jesus Anymore' and 'Ride 'em Jewboy'. Friedman used to comment that Jews and Texans were similar in that both wore hats indoors and both attached great significance to the fact. Freidman was very much a cult figure and his form of musical satire had a restricted following. In later years he turned to writing detective novels.
7. Sohn, A. (1998), 'Not mad about you: the Silver Jews' David Berman', *NYM Press, Arts and Listings*, October, 14.

Berman's comments are revealing. He is reclaiming Jewish identity. Black pride may have surfaced musically in the 1960s, but outward 'Jewish pride' has had to wait much longer in rock. But when it comes, so much has been lost.[8] Berman's lyrics contain few Jewish elements. There are no specifically Jewish echoes or allusions, as in Leonard Cohen's later 'Jewish blues'. Berman is not part of the Klezmer revival.[9] In fact, Berman himself seems to have little Jewish knowledge as such. He was raised in a secular — even anti-religious — family, living among non-Jews in Dallas.

The anthropologist, Thomas Fitzgerald, has suggested that much ethnic identification in contemporary America is devoid of substance. The old ways of life have passed. The younger generation, in an age of ethnic politics, take pride in identifying themselves with their ethnic roots while often knowing little about the heritage that their parents and grandparents had often tried to escape.[10] At best, a conscious effort has to be made to recover the past — as in the Jewish folklorism of the Klezmer movement or in Yiddish evening classes. Such an effort can be seen in Paul Simon's hiring of a genealogist to trace his family origins. The Yiddish phrases, gestures and turns of thought that the grandparents could not help using, often to the

---

8. By the same token, Jewish identity can be discussed and even mocked without necessarily evoking the traditions of anti-semitism. The punk-influenced American band NOFX on their recent live album have included a song 'We Are The Brews', which mocks the young Jews of Los Angeles. It is in bad taste, to be sure, but it does not have the force of discrimination behind it. It also has something that none of the classic Jewish pop writers have put into their work: Hebrew words. The song ends with the chant 'dyenu', taken from a traditional Passover song. I am grateful for the specialist knowledge of Ben Billig, who drew this example to my attention.
9. Not all of today's Klezmer's bands are narrowly folklorist. Some, like the Klezmatics, specifically combine traditional Klezmer music with more contemporary influences, including those from rock.
10. Fitzgerald, T.K. (1992) 'Media, ethnicity and identity' in *Culture and Power*, ed. P. Scannell, P. Schlesinger and C. Sparks. London: Sage. See also: Sollors W. (1986) *Beyond Ethnicity*. Oxford: Oxford University Press; Billig, M. (1995) *Banal Nationalism*. London: Sage.

embarrassment of their children, are disappearing, at least among secular families. The older generation have succeeded in turning their children and grandchildren into Americans, redefining the nature of American popular culture in the process. In doing this, something spontaneous and previously embarrassing, is lost. In the words of the (non-Jewish) songwriter Joni Mitchell, "you don't know what you've got, till it's gone". That is the paradox of much ethnic revival today.

A Golden Age?

Looking back on the Jewish contribution to rock, one can ask: where was the high spot, the supposed golden age? It is easy to point to the intellectual singer-songwriters. Unquestionably, original talents of the highest order are here. Lyrically, Dylan, Reed, Simon, Cohen and others were taking popular song into new areas. One could easily tell a story of the Jewish tradition of song-writing culminating in a burst of creative glory.

It would not be difficult, either, to connect this lyrical achievement to the importance of words in Jewish culture. After all, Jews, whether religious or secular, have traditionally been known as 'the People of the Book'.[11] There is also the tradition of Jewish humour. Much serious Talmudic scholarship depends on punning: the ability to look for alternative meanings of words is taught in traditional Hebrew classes. What is formally taught has also become a cultural habit. In the entertainment industry, there has been a long tradition of Jewish comedians — whether Jack Benny, Groucho Marx or Lenny Bruce — making the wry observations of the outsider, turning phrases on their head.

---

11. Heilman, S.C. (1983) *The People of the Book* Chicago: University of Chicago Press.

163

Jerry Leiber demonstrated how the one-liner can be used in the spare words of the rock lyric. Bob Dylan's recasting of the dialogue between God and Abe in the opening verse of 'Highway 61 Revisited' belongs to this tradition. Similarly, Lou Reed claimed his skill as a lyric writer was to be good at dialogue. Is it a surprise that a New York Jew should claim to have these skills?

The story could be told that Leiber, Stoller, Ragovoy, Pomus, Spector and all the others were a Jewish prelude for Dylan. Verse had become poetry. And with this move, popular music had come of age. That, however, would be a partial story. It would reflect the biases of a university education, which would see the rise of the intellectual as the culmination of pop history

However, there is another story to be told, that does not favour the intellectual over the popular. The high spot can be seen to have occurred just before the rise of the singer-songwriters, when Jews were still mainly confined to the backrooms of rock. This was when the Jewish soul men and the Brill writers were still co-operating with black musicians, in order to produce music that would cross racial lines. This very endeavour expresses, and reflects, the hopes of those times.

Toni Morrison, the distinguished black American novelist, has described the sixties as being "absolutely the finest decade" that America has ever known. It was a time when people "were questioning racial oppression in their own relationships".[12] Too often, analysts look to the late sixties and the culture of the hippies as the golden moment of the sixties. By this time, however, the music scene, at least in the United States, had fractured again along race lines. But perhaps one should look to the early sixties and to the music that intellectuals can so easily overlook as superficial

---

12. quoted in *Guardian*, 1998, March 24.

kitsch.[13] The Brill lyricists were not all da-doo-ron-ron. Something much more important is detectable in that work.

The philosopher Herbert Marcuse, who himself was a Jewish refugee from nazi Germany and who became a cult figure on radical campuses in the sixties, wrote that in every revolution there is a moment when the revolution could have been fully successful.[14] The moment passes and the revolutionary hopes are regularly betrayed. The civil rights movement, which in its early stages included a strong black-Jewish alliance, was to feel betrayed by the end of the sixties. If the revolutionary moment, of which Marcuse wrote, had a reflection in popular music, then this occurred in the early years of the decade. The youthful masses were listening collectively to music of optimism. The fact that black and whites were sharing the same experiences was, in itself, a marker for a future, which was never to come into being.

In this brief moment the Jewish role was crucial. Jewish songwriters, writing for black singers, were able to write in ways that seemed to speak directly to black audiences. Nelson George was quoted in an earlier chapter, praising the uncanny ability of Leiber and Stoller to write from the perspective of blacks. Similarly, Brian Ward, in *Just My Soul Responding*, mentions the ability of Leiber and Stoller and other white songwriters to write about black street life. Ward comments that they did so at a time when most black writers were cautious about addressing social issues directly: "White lyricists were among the most forthright in their portrayals of black, especially urban, life and its social, domestic and economic travails".[15]

---

13. For a discussion of the way that music scholars often dismiss popular music as *kitsch*, see: Denisoff, R.S. (1989) 'The evolution of pop music broadcasting: 1920-1972' in T.E. Scheurer (ed), *American Popular Music: Readings from the Popular Press Volume II: The Age of Rock*. Bowling Green, OH: Bowling Green State University Press.
14. Marcuse, H. (1969) *Eros and Civilization*. London: Sphere Books.
15. Ward, *Just My Soul Responding*, p214.

Ward's examples are 'Up On The Roof' (Goffin and King), 'Spanish Harlem' (Leiber and Spector) and 'A Quiet Place' (Ragovoy). He might just as well have added 'On Broadway' or a dozen Leiber and Stoller songs. In the same vein, Ward mentions white songwriters who had been able to express the romantic ideals in the black male psyche. He names Pomus, Shuman and Ragovoy.[16] He does not discuss the ethnic background of his exemplars. Just labelling them 'white' misses something of importance.

If one only sees the world in terms of black and white, then it is a mystery how such writers were able to evoke, to quote Ward again, "key aspects of the black mental and physical world".[17] In an obvious sense, the writers were not only evoking a black world. They were depicting their own world too. When B.B. King burst into tears, having recorded Doc Pomus's 'There Must Be A Better World Somewhere', he did not claim that the white songwriter had finally understood the black's singer's sensibilities. The movement of understanding was in the other direction. He declared that he finally understood what Doc was saying.

Similarly, 'Up On The Roof' and the other urban songs could not have worked unless they also expressed the authors' sensibilities. The writers lived in the city, suffered its heat. They came from backgrounds in which the degradations of prejudice and poverty were common folklore, if no longer everyday realities. Their own parents or grandparents would have had stories of pogroms and escape. The writers themselves, or their parents, had struggled out of urban ghettos.

The songs express the possibility of escape, through love, ambition or even just a climb onto the roof. Escape should not be confused with escapism. Nor should simplic-

---

16. Ward, p151.
17. Ward, p214.

ity be taken as simple-mindedness. These songs, and the moral vision they express, are not trivial. They capture the hope that escape is possible, and they did so at an important juncture of American history.

The moment of unity across the racial fault line did not last. With the advent of the Beatles and the singer songwriters, the pop lyric was freed from its earlier tight disciplines. But the freedom was also an ending, as well as a beginning. The mass audience began to fragment. When long-haired, mop-heads became fashionable, black singers like Ben E. King could no longer remain in the vanguard. African Americans could not take up the 'Beatles-look' hair-do. They were excluded by a fashion that was a white imperative.

The fault lines were always there, as they were in the historic alliance between Jews and blacks. So many songwriting Jews were on their way to positions of ownership in the music business. They were hiring the black singers. In response, black entrepreneurs were establishing their own labels, recruiting their own black singers. Increasingly, the next generation of Jews moved to the suburbs and to financial stability. The links with the urban ghettos were to be loosened. Both sides of the historic alliance cried betrayal.

Yet the brief moment has left an enduring legacy. Perhaps the musical peak was reached with Ben E. King's recording of 'Stand By Me', produced by Leiber and Stoller and written by all three. It is all there: the gospel influenced vocals, the hint of Latin rhythm, the imagery of the Jewish psalms, the violins (that most European of all instruments) — all delivered with hope. This music does not belong just to a single generation. It was a hit again in the 1980s, reaching number one in the UK singles charts. It will probably be revived in the future.

For 'Stand By Me', members of the century's two most oppressed minority groups combined their creative energies. In another art form, the collaboration might have appeared strained, or something to be openly commented upon. Imagine what would have been said at that time if blacks and Jews had collaborated on a play or a novel. And imagine how many intellectual commentaries would have subsequently been written.

For popular music of this type, the collaboration was natural and unremarkable. The resulting music spoke directly to millions, whatever their skin colour and religious background. To take the phrase of Doc Pomus, whose memory is for a blessing, 'this magic moment' may have passed; but it is recorded, to be enjoyed again and again. The enjoyment itself signals a hope for a better world, somewhere.

Index